WRITTEN IN HISTORY
Letters that Changed the World

▼

SIMON SEBAG
MONTEFIORE

WEIDENFELD & NICOLSON

First published in Great Britain in 2018 by Weidenfeld & Nicolson
This paperback edition published in 2019
by Weidenfeld & Nicolson
an imprint of The Orion Publishing Group Ltd
Carmelite House, 50 Victoria Embankment
London EC4Y 0DZ

An Hachette UK Company

1 3 5 7 9 10 8 6 4 2

A CIP catalogue record for this book
is available from the British Library.

ISBN (paperback) 9781474609197
ISBN (ebook) 9781474609203

Typeset by Input Data Services Ltd, Somerset

Printed and bound in Great Britain by Clays Ltd, Elcograf S.p.A.

www.weidenfeldandnicolson.co.uk
www.orionbooks.co.uk

To Lily Bathsheba

Contents

Blood

Destruction

Disaster

Friendship

Folly

Decency

Liberation

Fate

Power

Downfall

Goodbye

Introduction

Dear Reader,

Nothing beats the immediacy and authenticity of a letter. We humans have an instinct to record feelings and memories that could be lost in time, and to share them. We desperately need to confirm relationships, ties of love or hate, for the world is never still and our lives are a series of beginnings and endings: in recording them on paper, we perhaps feel we can make them more real, almost eternal. Letters are the literary antidote to the ephemerality of life and, of course, the flimsy fitfulness of the internet. Goethe, who reflected much on the magic of letters, thought them 'the most significant memorial a person can leave.' And those instincts are right: long after the protagonists are dead, letters live on. And in matters of politics, diplomacy and war, a command or a promise must be documented. So many different things are achieved through the medium of letters and we celebrate them all here.

There have been many collections of peculiar and funny letters, but these are chosen not just because they are entertaining but because they somehow changed human affairs, whether in war or peace, art or culture. They grant us a glimpse into fascinating lives, whether through the eyes of a genius, a monster or an ordinary person. Here are letters from many cultures, traditions, lands, races: ancient Egypt and Rome to modern America, Africa, India, China and Russia, where I have done a lot of my research and work – hence the presence here of many Russians from Pushkin to Stalin. Here, among other things, are struggles for rights that we now regard as essential, and orders for crimes we regard as intolerable. Here too are love letters and letters of power by empresses, actresses, tyrants, artists, composers, poets.

I have selected letters written by pharaohs three thousand years ago, preserved in forgotten libraries in fallen cities – and letters written this century. The letter certainly had a golden age: the five hundred years from the Middle Ages to widespread use of the telephone in the 1930s, declining steeply in the 1990s with the arrival of the mobile telephone and the internet. I saw it myself when I was researching in the Stalin archives. During the 1920s and 1930s, Stalin wrote long letters and notes to his entourage and to strangers too, particularly when he was on holiday in the south, but when a secure telephone line was set up, his letters abruptly stopped.

Letters were naturally widely used by rulers and elites soon after writing itself developed: they are the ideal tool of management and much, much more. During the last three millennia, letters were the equivalent of today's newspapers, telephones, radio, television, email, texting, sexting, and blogging all put together. This anthology contains letters originally written in cuneiform, the ancient system of writing using the markings of a reed stylus on a flattened moist clay tablet and dried in the sun, used in the Middle East during the Bronze and Iron Ages. And on papyrus, made with the pith of the papyrus plant, from the third millennium BC. And then letters written on parchment or vellum – the tougher, dried animal skin – until paper was created in China around 200 BC and gradually brought across central Asia to Europe. There, its cheaper and easier manufacture finally made it ever more convenient, available and affordable from the fifteenth century onwards. Letter-writing reached a climax between the fifteenth and early twentieth centuries not just because of the availability of paper, but also the easing of travel and distribution by courier, and the development of post.

It was also more than practical – it was part of a new state of order, of law and contract, responsible government, accountable finance and public morality. Above all, it was a new state of mind with fresh ideas and modern visions of how to live, an appreciation of privacy as well as a medium of promotion, and a growing sense of international society and personal consciousness.

Some letters were intended to act as publicity, some to remain absolutely secret. Their variety of usage is one of the joys of a collection like this. The vast majority of letters concerned mundane practicalities of little interest – ordering goods, paying bills, arranging meetings. At the height of letter-writing as art and tool, literate people spent many hours a day at their desks, sometimes in failing light, writing obsessively. Catherine the Great self-deprecatingly called herself a 'graphomaniac' (she also called herself a 'plantomaniac' for her love of gardening) and the only way to run an empire, a war, a state was to do so by frenzied letter-writing. It was a way for the writers to project their existence beyond their room, their house, village, country, to reach other worlds and distant dreams. It was a physically exhausting duty *and* a pastime; emails and texts are much less arduous to produce, but they are perhaps too easy, so informal that we don't respect the power of the words themselves, though of course brevity, speed and excitement make text as addictive as it is essential in all modern lives. Until the early twentieth century, few people, even heads of state, had offices to assist them with their vast correspondence and most of them answered and sealed (for security, partly) their own letters – including letter-writers who figure in this book such as Lincoln, Catherine and Nicholas II who actually stamped his own letters.

Of course, letter-writers don't always tell the truth in their letters and there can be an editing process in the choice of which letters they destroy and which they preserve. But either way, a letter reflects a single moment in time and experience – what Goethe called 'the immediate breath of life'. Many bonfires of letters were lit to destroy evidence of secret deals and forbidden loves. Such literary infernos happened frequently in Victorian and Edwardian families after the deaths of grandees – including in my own. But to destroy a letter, Goethe thought, even out of discretion, was destroying life itself.

History-writing – like contemporary journalism – is full of gossip, guesswork, mythology, lies, misunderstandings and calumnies. When we read a tabloid newspaper or a gossip site, we know that perhaps half of what we read is false: the joy of private letters is that they are the real thing. We are not depending on gossip: we can hear the authentic words. This is the way Stalin spoke to his henchmen; the way Hurrem talked lovingly to Suleiman the Magnificent or Frida Kahlo to Diego Rivera; and then of course there are Mozart's outrageously scatological letters to his cousin Marianne.

These letters fall into various types. First: public letters. Mao Zedong launches the Cultural Revolution with a letter to students ordering them to attack their superiors; Balfour promises a Jewish homeland; Émile Zola's letter 'J'Accuse!' confronts France about its racism and antisemitism. In the twenty-first century, I am afraid such a protest feels horribly contemporary – and absolutely necessary in our new venomous age of antisemitism on both sides of the Atlantic, not just from the right but increasingly, particularly in Britain, from the mainstream socialist left, a vile strain leading straight back to Stalin's antisemitic purges. But it also goes further back too: Marxism is in fashion again. I have added some priceless letters between the two creators of Marxism, Karl Marx and Friedrich Engels, whose vicious and shameless racism and antisemitism may surprise those who regard them as selfless and noble campaigners for ordinary decency and equality. Far from it, their letters are peppered with words like 'nigger' and 'Yid' and reflections on the Jewish member of their rival Lassalle. These may shock some readers.

In the centuries before the popularity of the press, many

letters were designed to be copied out and widely distributed in society. Thus the public letters of great correspondents such as Voltaire and Catherine the Great were enjoyed in literary salons across Europe. Similarly with another sort of official letter: the announcement of a military victory or defeat. Even at the end of battles, when the fields were strewn with bodies quivering and shattered, exhausted generals would sit down in ruined cottages or at makeshift open-air desks to write letters throughout the night to announce their victories to the world. After the victories of Poltava, Austerlitz and Blenheim, Peter the Great, Napoleon and Marlborough announce their news to the world – though they also boast privately to their lovers and wives. 'Come and celebrate with me!' writes Peter the Great to his wife.

Until recently, all negotiations or commands, particularly political or military ones, would be borne in letters *not* to be read by the public. Here is Rameses the Great's disdainful note to the Hittite king Hattusili. A millennium after that, Mark Antony writes to Octavian (the future emperor Augustus) to complain that his 'screwing' Cleopatra is not politically significant – even though it clearly is. Leap a millennium again: Saladin and Richard the Lionheart negotiate to partition the Holy Land. Then forward another five hundred years: Philip II is ordering his admiral Medina Sidonia to command the Armada against England – even though the latter believes the enterprise will fail. Another four centuries and we are admiring Lincoln's generosity of spirit in a letter to General Grant. And there is no more important correspondence in the twentieth century than that between Roosevelt and Churchill during the desperate months of 1940. On the night before he invades Soviet Russia, Hitler reveals his motives in a letter to his ally Mussolini at the height of his hubristic swagger. And there's one letter here that was never sent: Eisenhower's draft addressed to the troops, if D-Day fails.

Then there is a special sort of letter that is both political and personal – and these are especially relevant in autocracies, where the intimate life of the ruler is political. As we can see in many of the new autocracies of the twenty-first century, when the ruler is absolute, everything personal is political. Henry VIII's love letter to Anne Boleyn and James I's to his handsome male favourite, the Duke of Buckingham are of political importance – the ruler's amorous preferences guide national government. The repulsive entertainments, usually involving anuses and sausages, laid on for Kaiser Wilhelm II by his courtiers reveal the coarse incompetence that threatened European peace. Catherine the Great and Prince Potemkin, lovers as well as political partners, are passionate romantics yet clear-eyed politicians. Among their letters are some, ten to fifteen pages long, that discuss every aspect of power – diplomacy, war, finance, personnel. But they also cover domestic matters – art-collecting, building houses, their sexual affairs and of course their health: no eighteenth-century letter is complete without a discussion of haemorrhoids. But their short love letters resemble modern emails or texts. Letters like these were never meant to be read by anyone but the recipients, but most were kept after their deaths. Potemkin died on a wild steppe in Moldova gripping a packet of Catherine's letters, wrapped in a ribbon, weeping as he read them.

Such *really* private correspondence celebrates love and sex, but these were letters that their writers kept under lock and key. Alexander II and his mistress (later wife) Katya exchange the most erotic letters ever written by a head of state. At the time they would have presumed that no one would ever see them – yet here we are, reading the letters of Vita Sackville-West and Virginia Woolf; Napoleon and Josephine; Emma Hamilton and Nelson. Balzac's correspondence with his Polish fan, the beautiful Countess Hánska, is so fervent, they fall in love before they meet – just by the power of letters. Anaïs Nin's correspondence with Henry Miller is so ablaze with sexuality, so awash with lubricity, it almost tastes of carnality. 'More than kisses', wrote John Donne, 'letters mingle souls.' And bodies.

Naturally I have chosen intimate letters of pain as well as pleasure, of the end of love as well as the beginning: one of the most remarkable and little known is Thomas Jefferson's 'conversation' between his Head and his Heart, sent to his young mistress who is leaving him. It must be one of the most brilliant analyses of the craziness of love ever written – and the acuity is not surprising because this is the author of the American Declaration of Independence.

Similarly, Simón Bolívar tries to end his affair with the fabulous Manuela Sáenz. The married beauty Henriette, returning to her husband, breaks the heart of the quintessential womaniser, Casanova. Just before his own death, Leonard Cohen wishes farewell to his dying lover who inspired his greatest songs including 'So Long, Marianne'. My favourite goodbye is the letter of the triumphant Caliph of Islamic Spain, Abd-al Rahman III, who reflects on his deathbed that, out of fifty years of glory, he has enjoyed just fourteen days of happiness. And few letters are more heartbreaking than Alan Turing's agony over the persecution of his homosexuality. And of course there is the unbearable horror of a rare goodbye letter from wife to husband within the death camps of the Holocaust.

Some of these letters recount great events or spectacles – Columbus reports to his monarchs on the 'discovery' of America; the Battle of Britain is recounted in a young pilot's letter to his parents. It's especially poignant because the pilot is killed soon afterwards. Chekhov observes the suffering of the desperate criminals of Sakhalin. Pliny sees the destruction of Pompeii. Voltaire reflects on the Lisbon earthquake of 1755.

A subset of what we might call tourism tells of sexual adventures in interesting places, a popular type of letter in the eighteenth and nineteenth centuries, when the modern experience of travel as leisure expanded from the Grand Tours of wealthy aristocrats to middle-class travel by train, shrinking the world in a way never before achieved: Chekhov and Flaubert cheerfully describe encounters with Japanese prostitutes and Egyptian youths in beautiful prose.

Then there are letters of family, where we witness the intimate relationships of great men with their children such as these two Mughal emperors: Babur advises his son on tolerance. Aurangzeb writes to his son from his deathbed as his empire falls apart. As he awaits his own trial, Charles I tells his son how to be a king. Empress Maria Theresa warns her daughter Queen Marie Antoinette that her arrogance will destroy her. Or the other way around: Svetlana Stalina plays at being the dictator and gives orders to her father – including one to ban homework in the entire Soviet Union for a year. There is also the awkwardness of families, which among royalty is magnified to epic proportions. The future Queen Elizabeth I begs for her life from her sister Queen 'Bloody' Mary. Joseph II comes to Paris as sex adviser to his sister Marie Antoinette, when Louis XVI is unable to consummate their marriage.

The anonymous warning of the Gunpowder Plot is itself decisive in defeating the conspiracy – it changes history at a stroke. Rasputin in his letter to Nicholas II tries to stop the First World War breaking out, but fails. Some of the letters are themselves orders to kill: Stalin's notes encourage his secret policemen to execute 'enemies' who are actually innocent, and Lenin frenziedly orders executions of random victims. Three thousand years ago, an Egyptian ruler tells his wife to murder two junior officials and 'disappear' their bodies. One of my favourites is Tito's laconic note to Stalin, threatening to send an assassin if Stalin tries to kill him again.

One special category covers self-destruction: Oscar Wilde receives the insulting letter from his lover's father calling him a 'Somdomite'; Alexander Hamilton and Alexander Pushkin write their way towards the duels that kill them. Another particular species of letter is the last goodbye: for instance, Sir Walter Raleigh's letter to his wife before his execution. Emperor Hadrian, realising he is dying, writes to his adopted son and successor Antoninus Pius. Bolívar, ailing and exhausted, damns the Americas. Kafka orders his works destroyed. And it is not just Kafka who doubts the value of his works: another theme is the torment and disappointment of creativity seen in such letters as Keats' on love and death; Michelangelo's stress as he paints the Sistine Chapel; or T.S. Eliot turning down George Orwell's new novel *Animal Farm*.

Here you will also read timeless letters that tell of the brave struggles for freedom in the modern era, such as the liberation of slaves, votes for women and African-American civil rights. Toussaint L'Ouverture, who has led the Haitian slave revolt against the French that leads to the first independent black republic of the Americas, now begs for his family's life. Nelson Mandela tells his wife Winnie how to live with hope, even inside a prison cell. Rosa Parks challenges racial segregation in Alabama. Abram Hannibal, a slave captured, probably, in West Africa, then sold to the slave markets of Istanbul and on to the Russian tsar, becomes the first black general in Europe. Gifted women defy their shackles: Ada Lovelace writes about her love of science; Fanny Burney and Manuela Sáenz defy the necessity of boring, male-centred marriage; Emmeline Pankhurst defends violent action in order to win the vote for women.

Email and the telephone may have ended the golden age of letters, but they have kept their power – for example, in diplomacy. In 2018, when President Donald Trump cancels his planned Singapore summit with the young and murderous North Korean dictator Kim Jong Un he does so in a very Trumpian letter. It sparks an energetic correspondence. The summit takes place in Singapore after all. A few days later, on 6 July, Chairman Kim writes to Trump: 'The significant first meeting with Your Excellency was indeed the start of a meaningful journey.' Trump soon went further, boasting to a rally about his North Korean epistolary affair: 'I was being really tough and so was he. We would go back and forth. And then we fell in love, OK? No, really – he wrote me beautiful letters and they're great letters.' Whatever the future of North Korean nuclear weapons, this at least proves the emotional and political power of the letter.

While on the subject of the new brazen, vicious age of authoritarian swagger, ruthless bombast and vicious hostility in public life, personified by Trump's presidency, I have added to this paperback, the charming, elegant letter left by President George H.W. Bush (who had called for a 'kinder gentler' politics) for his successor, Bill Clinton in the Oval Office: it neatly and warmly puts aside petty insecurity and political malice to celebrate their shared American ideal. That's a sentiment sadly missing today.

Letters are returning to favour among those looking to be more discreet in their communication. Politicians, spies, criminals and lovers have all learned, many the hard way, that emails and texts can be read and exposed; they are never destroyed. But they often vanish. Their impermanence makes them unsatisfying as a medium. They make life feel more transient while letters make it feel more enduring. Even the most heavily encrypted messages can be decrypted. Intelligence services like the CIA, GCHQ or FSB, aided by renegade ghostly armies of plundering freelance hackers, are harvesting vast caches of messages. For this reason, people are starting to use pen and paper again, especially in government: letters can be preserved, but ironically they are safer, because they exist only once and can be physically destroyed. Top Russian officials now tell me that in the Kremlin today, all affairs of any importance are conducted by letter and note, on old-fashioned paper, with traditional ink or lead, nib or ballpoint, despatched by loyal courier. No more sleek electronic devices! We should take note: no one knows like the Kremlin court of President Putin, that crenelated hive of cyber espionage, how insecure and dangerous are those easy texts and swift emails. Yet, as this anthology shows, letters often have a much longer life than their writers ever imagined.

I hope the readers of this collection wonder at the bravery, beauty and visceral authenticity of these letters. While the surfer of the internet feels more alone than ever amidst invisible millions, the writer of a single letter to a correspondent is never lonely. Lord Byron, whose daughter Ada appears in this anthology, understood this when he mused that 'letter-writing is the only device combining solitude and good company', for the letter-writer is enriched by the sensation of warmth that someone far away will soon share his or her sentiments. May it encourage you to write your own letters, inspired by the brilliance of these examples of the art.

Yours sincerely,

Simon Sebag Montefiore
May 2019

P.S. I hope you may also enjoy the companion volume of this book: *Voices of History: Speeches that Changed the World*.

P.P.S. In some cases, where the texts are too long, the detail too obscure or the sex too repetitive, I have edited letters for the ease of the reader. Also, I have used the regnant names for all ruling monarchs, even if they were not yet sovereigns at the time of writing. This is to make it easy to recognise them: Elizabeth I was a princess of dubious prospects when she wrote the Tide Letter to Queen Mary – but the letter appears in the List of Contents as 'Elizabeth I to Mary I'. Apologies if this bothers anyone.

Love

Henry VIII to Anne Boleyn, May 1528

This is one of the love letters that changed history. Henry was the second son of Henry VII, who had seized the throne for his new-fangled Tudor dynasty in 1485. Only the death of his elder brother Prince Arthur brought Henry VIII to the throne, in 1509. Arthur left a young widow, Catherine of Aragon, daughter of the Spanish monarchs. On his accession, Henry suddenly decided to marry Catherine. Now, almost twenty years into their marriage, the king desperately needed a male heir. So far, only a daughter, Mary, had survived. After an affair with a young courtier named Mary Boleyn, he started to notice her sister, Anne, a lady-in-waiting to the queen. By 1528 Henry is in love with Anne Boleyn, eleven years younger than him. Although it is unlikely that their love affair has yet been consummated, he is already utterly enraptured by her. She is resisting his attempts at seduction. Her mix of chastity, sophistication, her ambition to marry the king, not be seduced like her sister, and her cool, haughty allure intensify Henry's fervour. Her personality makes him doubt her love – 'I hope on yours also' – but later he would bitterly resent her wiles and take a terrible revenge.

Henry's love dovetailed with his conviction that his entire marriage to Catherine was incestuous and that divine displeasure was the cause of his lack of sons. He therefore ordered his ministers to secure an annulment from the Pope. But the Catholic Church would deny Henry's wishes in his Great Matter, which would lead to England's decisive break with Rome and the establishment of the Church of England; and in turn this allowed him to marry Anne in 1532. When Anne produced a daughter, the future Elizabeth I, but no sons, Henry turned on her: she was executed in 1536.

My mistress and friend: I and my heart put ourselves in your hands, begging you to have them suitors for your good favour, and that your affection for them should not grow less through absence. For it would be a great pity to increase their sorrow since absence does it sufficiently, and more than ever I could have thought possible reminding us of a point in astronomy, which is, that the longer the days are the farther off is the sun, and yet the more fierce. So it is with our love, for by absence we are parted, yet nevertheless it keeps its fervour, at least on my side, and I hope on yours also: assuring you that on my side the ennui of absence is already too much for me: and when I think of the increase of what I must needs suffer it would be well nigh unbearable for me were it not for the firm hope I have and as I cannot be with you in person, I am sending you the nearest possible thing to that, namely, my picture set in a bracelet, with the whole device which you already know. Wishing myself in their place when it shall please you. This by the hand of

Your loyal servant and friend

H. Rex

Frida Kahlo to Diego Rivera, undated

Frida Kahlo's love letters to her husband, the painter Diego Rivera, are filled with the bold colours and wild passions of her art – and her life. Born of a German father and a Mexican mother in 1907, she was almost crippled by polio and was then terribly injured in a near-fatal bus accident in 1927. An iron rod had penetrated her uterus. She spent three months in a full-body cast and endured thirty operations and a lifetime of pain. While recovering, she started to paint and encountered Diego, already famous; both were leftists and they met through the Communist Party. Diego became her artistic mentor. Rivera had lived in Paris, travelled in Italy and evolved his own style of murals, bold in colour, his figures almost Aztec in their simplicity, all telling the history of Mexico and its revolution. Diego and Frida became lovers: he was forty-two, she twenty.

Kahlo and Rivera married in 1929, but the marriage was tempestuous.

He was foul-tempered and an enthusiastic womaniser and she had affairs with men, including the Russian revolutionary leader in exile Leon
Trotsky, as well as with women such as the French-American singer
and dancer Josephine Baker. Neither her health problems nor the
conservative Catholicism of much of Mexican society prevented her
developing her artistic vision, her elaborate colourful costumes showing her mixed-race heritage, her liberated love life. Kahlo's dramatic
artistic style, a flamboyant mix of fantastical and realistic, magical and
folk, was inspired by both Mexico itself and her own extraordinary life.
All of this is revealed in her letters to Rivera, in which physical love and
emotional turbulence are often expressed in the colours of a painter:
'the silent life giver of worlds, what is most important is the nonillusion.
morning breaks, the friendly reds, the big blues, hands full of leaves,
noisy birds, fingers in the hair, pigeons' nests a rare understanding of
human struggle simplicity of the senseless song the folly of the wind
in my heart = don't let them rhyme girl = sweet xocolatl [chocolate] of
ancient Mexico, storm in the blood that comes in through the mouth –
convulsion, omen, laughter and sheer teeth needles of pearl, for some
gift on a seventh of July, I ask for it, I get it, I sing, sang, I'll sing from
now on our magic – lo'. She describes their love in terms of Mexican
landscape, and even fruit: 'it was the thirst of many years restrained in
your body . . . There was all manner of fruits in the juice of your lips, the
blood of pomegranate, the horizon of the mammee and the purified
pineapple. I pressed you against my breast and the prodigy of your
form penetrated my book through the tips of my fingers. Smell of oak
essence, memories of walnut, green breath of ash tree. Horizon and
landscapes, I trace them with a kiss . . . I penetrate the sex of the whole
earth, her heat chars me and my entire body is rubbed by the freshness
of the tender leaves.'

They divorced in 1939. For a long time, she was known mainly as
Diego's wife – but now the paintings of Frida and the huge, exuberant
murals of her husband form the national art of Mexico. As for their
volcanic relationship, she put it best: 'only one mountain can know the
core of another mountain.'

Diego:

Nothing compares to your hands, nothing like the green-gold of your eyes. My body is filled with you for days and days. you are the mirror of the night. the violent flash of lightning. the dampness of the earth. The hollow of your armpits is my shelter. my fingers touch your blood. All my joy is to feel life spring from your flower-fountain that mine keeps to fill all the paths of my nerves which are yours.

Thomas Jefferson to Maria Cosway, 12 October 1786

He is the American ambassador to Paris. She is 'a golden-haired, languishing Anglo-Italian, graceful . . . and highly accomplished, especially in music'. He is forty-three, she is twenty-seven. He is a widower, she is married. Jefferson, born in Virginia, was a wealthy landowner who, in 1776, had drafted the Declaration of Independence of the new nation of America. Born near Florence in 1759, Maria Cosway was the daughter of an expatriate English innkeeper and the wife of an eccentric painter. In Paris, during autumn 1786, Maria and Jefferson have spent an intense month in each other's company.

When she leaves, Jefferson writes her this extraordinary letter in which one of the reigning intellects of Western history applies himself to the dilemma of love, to heartbreak and to human nature. To be in love, to drink the elixir of loving, he argues, is worth the inevitable heartbreak. And America would not have been liberated without the passion of the heart. His conclusion? 'We have no rose without its thorn'. They never meet again, but correspond for the rest of their lives.

Soon after Maria leaves, Jefferson is joined in Paris by his daughter and her mixed-race slave companion, Sally Heming, sixteen, with whom Jefferson begins a relationship that would produce at least five children. In 1790, Jefferson returned home to become the first Secretary of State in President Washington's cabinet and was elected the third

President in 1801. Here is this very special letter that expresses the agonies and dilemmas of any man or woman unsuitably in love.

Seated by my fireside solitary and sad, the following dialogue took place between my Head and my Heart.

Head. Well, friend, you seem to be in a pretty trim.

Heart. I am indeed the most wretched of all earthly beings. Overwhelmed with grief, every fiber of my frame distended beyond its natural powers to bear, I would willingly meet whatever catastrophe should leave me no more to feel or to fear.

Head. These are the eternal consequences of your warmth and precipitation. This is one of the scrapes into which you are ever leading us. You confess your follies indeed: but you still hug and cherish them; and no reformation can be hoped, where there is no repentance.

Heart. Oh my friend! This is no moment to upbraid my foibles. I am rent into fragments by the force of my grief! If you have any balm, pour it into my wounds: if none, do not harrow them by new torments. Spare me in this awful moment! At any other I will attend with patience to your admonitions.

Head. On the contrary I never found that the moment of triumph with you was the moment of attention to my admonitions. While suffering under your follies you may perhaps be made sensible of them, but, the paroxysm over, you fancy it can never return. Harsh therefore as the medicine may be, it is my office to administer it . . .

Heart. May heaven abandon me if I do! . . .

Head. I wished to make you sensible how imprudent it is
to place your affections, without reserve, on objects you
must so soon lose and whose loss when it comes must cost
you such severe pangs. Remember the last night. You knew
your friends were to leave Paris today. This was enough to
throw you into agonies. All night you tossed us from one
side of the bed to the other. No sleep, no rest . . . To avoid
these eternal distresses, to which you are forever exposing
us, you must learn to look forward before each step which
may interest our peace. Everything in this world [is] a
matter of calculation. Advance then with caution, the
balance in your hand. Put into one scale the pleasures
which any object may offer; but put fairly into the other
the pains which are to follow, and see which preponder-
ates. The making [of] an acquaintance is not a matter of
indifference. When a new one is proposed to you, view it
all round. Consider what advantages it presents, and what
inconveniences it may expose you. Do not bite at the bait
of pleasure till you know there is no hook beneath it. The
art of life is the art of avoiding pain: and he is the best pilot
who steers clearest of the rocks and shoals with which he
is beset. Pleasure is always before us; but misfortune is at
our side: while running after that, this arrests us. The most
effectual means of being secure against pain is to retire
within ourselves, and to suffice for our own happiness . . .

Heart. And what more sublime delight than to mingle tears
with one whom the hand of heaven hath smitten! To watch
over the bed of sickness, and to beguile its tedious and its
painful moments! To share our bread with one to whom
misfortune has left none! This world abounds indeed with
misery; to lighten its burdens we must divide it with one
another . . . When nature assigned us the same habitation,

she gave us over it a divided empire. To you she allotted the
field of science, to me that of morals. When the circle is to
be squared, or the orbit of a comet to be traced; when the
arch of greatest strength, or the solid of least resistance
is to be investigated, take you the problem: it is yours;
nature has given me no cognizance of it. In like manner in
denying to you the feelings of sympathy, of benevolence,
of gratitude, of justice, of love, of friendship, she has
excluded you from their control. To these she has adapted
the mechanism of the heart. Morals were too essential to
the happiness of man to be risked on the uncertain combi-
nations of the head. She laid their foundation therefore in
sentiment, not science. That she gave to all, as necessary to
all: this to a few only, as sufficing with a few. I know indeed
that you pretend authority to the sovereign control of our
conduct in all its parts: and a respect for your grave saws
and maxims, a desire to do what is right, has sometimes
induced me to conform to your counsels . . . If our country,
when pressed with wrongs at the point of a bayonet had
been governed by its heads instead of its hearts, where
should we have been now? Hanging on a gallows as
high as Haman's. You began to calculate and to compare
wealth and numbers: we threw up a few pulsations of our
warmest blood: we supplied enthusiasm against wealth
and numbers: we put our existence to the hazard, when
the hazard seemed against us, and we saved our country:
justifying at the same time the ways of Providence, whose
precept is to do always what is right, and leave the issue to
him. In short, my friend, as far as my recollection serves
me, I do not know that I ever did a good thing on your
suggestion, or a dirty one without it. I do forever then
disclaim your interference in my province. Fill paper as
you please with triangles and squares: try how many ways
you can hang and combine them together . . . We are not

immortal ourselves, my friend; how can we expect our enjoyments to be so? We have no rose without its thorn; no pleasure without alloy. It is the law of our existence; and we must acquiesce.

Catherine the Great to Prince Potemkin, c.19 March 1774

This is the letter that reveals one of the most successful romantic partnerships and political alliances in all of history. Catherine was brought to Russia as a young German princess to marry the poxy heir to the throne, Grand Duke Peter, an inadequate bully who made her life hell. She was clever, cultured, passionate and ambitious. Desperately lonely, she was supported personally and politically by a series of lovers. When it had become clear that her husband, as Emperor Peter III, was both a disastrous tsar and a dangerous man, she overthrew him with the aid of her lover, Orlov, and made herself Catherine II. Peter III was strangled. In danger of being murdered herself, Catherine was scarcely helped by Orlov. When their relationship founders, his replacement is an intellectual non-entity named Vasilchikov, who makes her even more unhappy. She needs the support of an equal, and she knows Grigory Potemkin already. Brilliant, flamboyant and masterful, he is already in love with her.

Now she falls in love with him, knowing he has an intellect as superb as hers. In their letters, they call each other 'twin souls', writing day and night. Sometimes her letters are like texts: 'Me love general, general love me', but their ambitions are imperial. Physical passion dovetails with political acumen, and changes Russia's history: together they expand into Ukraine, annex Crimea, and found a Black Sea fleet as well as new cities from Odessa to Kherson.

In this letter, Catherine, nicknaming Potemkin 'my hero', 'a Cossack' and a Muslim Tatar (a 'giaour'), admits that even at dawn, after a row in which she decides to break up, she cannot live without the charismatic Potemkin: she is overcome with love and lust – what has he done to the cleverest woman in Europe?

Darling, really now, I suppose you thought I wouldn't write to you today. You're quite mistaken, sir. I awoke at five o'clock, it's now after six – I should write to him [Vasilchikov]. But only so much as to speak the truth, and kindly take heed what sort of truth: I don't love you and don't want to see you anymore. You won't believe it, my love, but I can't abide you at all. Yesterday we chatted till twelve o'clock, and then he was sent away. Don't be angry – indeed, as if one couldn't do without him. The dearest thing of all that came from that conversation is that I learned what they say among themselves: no, they say, this is no Vasilchikov, this one she treats differently. And he is indeed worthy. No one is surprised, and the affair has been accepted as if they have long been expecting it. But no – everything must be otherwise. From my pinky to my heel and from these to the last hair on my head, I have issued a general prohibition today against showing you the least affection. And my love is being kept in my heart under lock and key. It's awful how cramped it is in there. With great difficulty it squeezes itself inside, so mind well – it might just pop out somewhere. Now see here, you are a reasonable man, could so few lines contain more madness? A flood of foolish words has sprung from my head. How you can enjoy spending time with such a deranged mind I do not know. Oh, Mister Potemkin, what strange miracle have you performed in so thoroughly deranging a head that earlier was considered by society to be one of the best in Europe?

It's time, high time indeed to start acting sensibly. It's shameful, it's bad, it's a sin for Catherine the Second to allow this mad passion to rule over her. Such foolhardiness will make you loathsome even to him. I'll begin repeating that last verse to myself often, and I hope this alone will be enough to lead me back onto the true path. But this won't be the final proof of your great power over me. It's time to stop or I'll scribble a complete sentimental metaphysics that will finally make you laugh, though this will be its sole benefit. Well, my nonsense, off you go to those places, those happy shores where my hero dwells. If, perchance, you don't find him still at home and are carried back to me, then I shall toss you directly into the fire and Grishenka won't see this extravagant behaviour, in which, however, God knows, there is much love; but it would be much better if he didn't know of this.

Farewell, giaour, Muscovite, Cossack. I don't love you.

James I to George Villiers, Duke of Buckingham, 17 May 1620

This is a love letter from the married King James I to his adored male favourite. James had a history of intimate relationships with handsome young men. From the moment James saw George Villiers in 1614, aged twenty-one, he was dazzled by the youth's physical beauty, and he turned out to be intelligent too, if not especially talented. Appointed the king's cupbearer, he was swiftly promoted all the way up the peerage to Duke of Buckingham (1623) – and effectively chief minister as Lord High Admiral – making him the most hated man in the kingdom.

James publicly kissed and caressed George, whom he lovingly called 'Steenie' because St Stephen had 'the face of an angel', and he admitted in 1617 to the Council 'you may be sure that I love the Earl of Buckingham more than anyone else ... I wish ... not to have it thought to be a defect, for Jesus Christ did the same, and therefore I cannot be blamed. Christ had John, and I have George.' There was probably some sexual relationship: Buckingham reminisced in a letter to James 'whether you loved me now ... better than at the time which I shall never forget at Farnham, where the bed's head could not be found between the master and his dog'. James called Buckingham his wife: 'God bless you, my sweet child and wife, and grant that ye may ever be a comfort to your dear father and husband.' Remarkably, Buckingham also managed to become best friends with James's son and heir Charles I. He remained on top after James's death. But in 1628, he was assassinated by a disgruntled officer. In this letter written at the height of his power, James has helped him make a rich marriage to Lady Katherine Manners, but even after the wedding, he still praises Buckingham's 'white teeth'.

My only sweet and dear child,

Thy dear dad sends thee his blessing this morning and also to his daughter. The Lord of Heaven send you a sweet and blithe wakening, all kind of comfort in your sanctified bed, and bless the fruits thereof that I may have sweet bedchamber boys to play me with, and this is my daily prayer, sweet heart. When thou risest, keep thee from importunity of people that may trouble thy mind, that at meeting I may see thy white teeth shine upon me, and so bear me comfortable company in my journey. And so God bless thee, hoping thou will not forget to read over again my former letter.

James R.

Vita Sackville-West to Virginia Woolf, 21 January 1926

Vita Sackville-West was an aristocratic poet and novelist, daughter of Lord Sackville. After she married the diplomat Harold Nicolson in 1913 she continued to have love affairs with women, and perhaps the greatest love of her life was with the novelist Virginia Woolf. In February 1923, Woolf wrote in her diary: '[Vita] is a practised Sapphist & may ... have an eye on me, old though I am.' Virginia, neé Stephens and married to Leonard Woolf, was then forty-four, ten years older than Vita. Virginia considered herself provincial and dowdy by comparison with Vita's flamboyant libertinism, as well as less successful as a writer.

Vita admired Virginia's 'exquisite' writing. In this unshowy love letter, Sackville-West, writing to Woolf from one of her Italian retreats in early 1926, reassures her lover of her affections, even though she has other lovers. The relationship was over by 1928, but it inspired Woolf's novel *Orlando* which, with its recognisable gender-switching protagonist, is in some ways Virginia's love letter to Vita.

Milan
Thursday, January 21, 1926

I am reduced to a thing that wants Virginia. I composed a beautiful letter to you in the sleepless nightmare hours of the night, and it has all gone: I just miss you, in a quite simple desperate human way. You, with all your un-dumb letters, would never write so elementary a phrase as that; perhaps you wouldn't even feel it. And yet I believe you'll be sensible of a little gap. But you'd clothe it in so exquisite a phrase that it would lose a little of its reality. Whereas with me it is quite stark: I miss you even more than I could have believed; and I was prepared to miss you a good deal. So this letter is just really a squeal of pain. It is incredible how essential to me you have become. I suppose you are accustomed to people saying these things. Damn you, spoilt creature; I shan't make you love me any the more by giving myself away like this – But oh my dear, I can't be clever and stand-offish with you: I love you too much for that. Too truly. You have no idea how stand-offish I can be with people I don't love. I have brought it to a fine art. But you have broken down my defences. And I don't really resent it . . .

Please forgive me for writing such a miserable letter.
V.

Between Suleiman the Magnificent and Hurrem Sultan, c.1530s

These two love letters tell the story of the partnership of a slave girl and the most powerful monarch in the world. She was probably a blonde Russian priest's daughter, a Christian, who was captured and sold into the harem of the Ottoman sultan Suleiman the Magnificent, who ruled for forty-six years from 1520. She was obviously a remarkable character of force and intelligence. Although he had access to thousands of odalisques in the harem and already had a consort who had given him a son and heir, Prince Mustafa, Suleiman fell in love with Roxelana, giving her the new name Hurrem, 'Delight', for her exuberance and 'eyes full of mischief'.

Ottoman padishahs wrote love poetry using noms de plume, and Suleiman, often away fighting the Hungarians or the Persians, wrote Hurrem poems under the name Muhibbi. Here is one of his verses that are still celebrated.

Suleiman to Hurrem

Throne of my lonely niche, my wealth, my love, my moonlight.
My most sincere friend, my confidante, my very existence, my Sultan
The most beautiful among the beautiful . . .
My springtime, my merry faced love, my daytime, my sweetheart, laughing leaf . . .
My plants, my sweet, my rose, the one only who does not distress me in this world . . .
My Istanbul, my Caraman, the earth of my Anatolia
My Badakhshan, my Baghdad, my Khorasan
My woman of the beautiful hair, my love of the slanted

brow, my love of eyes full of mischief . . . .
I'll sing your praises always
I, lover of the tormented heart, Muhibbi of the eyes full of
tears, I am happy

Around 1521, Hurrem gave birth to a first son – the essential male heir. Suleiman ignored the restriction of one son to each concubine, and around 1533, he married her, breaking the precedent that sultans didn't wed concubines. Hurrem had the luck to give her emperor five sons and a daughter, mentioned in this letter. Most lived long lives – especially their beautiful and intelligent daughter Mihrimah, who became her father's trusted aide and the adviser to her brother Selim too. Over the years, Hurrem proved a formidable politician, challenging the monarch's eldest son Mustafa, who was strangled on the orders of his father. Hurrem died in 1558, before Suleiman, but she managed to contrive the succession in 1566 of her son Selim. Hurrem's domed tomb stands next to Suleiman's in the Süleymaniye Mosque, Istanbul. Here is one of Hurren's letters to Suleiman on campaign:

Hurrem to Suleiman

My Sultan, there is no limit to the burning anguish of separation. Now spare this miserable one and do not withhold your noble letters. Let my soul gain at least some comfort from a letter . . . When your noble letters are read, your servant and son Mir Mehmed and your slave and daughter Mihrimah weep and wail from missing you. Their weeping has driven me mad, it is as if we were in mourning. My Sultan, your son Mir Mehmed and your daughter Mihrimah and Selim Khan and Abdullah send you many greetings and rub their faces in the dust at your feet.

Anaïs Nin to Henry Miller, c. August 1932

Born in France in 1903 to Cuban parents, Anaïs Nin gave new expression
to female power, freedom and eroticism as well as to female suffering
from male abuse. She kept diaries that recorded her incestuous, abu-
sive relationship with her father, then as she grew up she celebrated her
own sensibilities, literary, emotional and erotic. Living with her Scottish
banker husband Hugh Guiler in Paris in the 1930s, she was writing
essays and stories but putting her talent into her diaries.

The American writer Henry Miller, nicknamed 'the gangster author',
was living hand-to-mouth in Paris while he completed the first of his
erotic, ribaldly Rabelaisian, masculine masterpieces, Tropic of Cancer. But
both lived for writing – 'at the core of us is a writer, not a human being,'
Nin wrote. He was thirty-nine, penniless and married to his second wife
June Smith, a fascinating, secretive beauty, when he came for lunch at
the Guilers. He came alone – June was still in New York.

Nin, aged twenty-nine, first becomes obsessed with Miller as a
writer. When she meets his wife June, the two women have a short
affair. Then Anaïs and Henry embark on their own voyage of sex and
literature. He admires her diary and stories; she recognises the greatness of his novels Tropic of Cancer and Tropic of Capricorn, in which June
appears as the femme fatale, Mona/Mara. Nin and her husband paid
for their publication. Their affair was always adventurously erotic and
also a celebration of life. 'He is a man who life makes drunk,' she wrote,
'like me.' But after making love, they discussed books at length: 'Henry
used my love well, beautifully – he erected books with it.'

Theirs is one of the best romantic correspondences – sexy, messy,
uninhibited, poetical, beautifully written, unhinged: 'Anaïs', he writes
in the summer of 1932, 'Here is the first woman with whom I can be
absolutely sincere . . . I mean I can never be absolutely loyal – it's not
in me – I love women or life too much . . . But laugh Anaïs . . . I love to
hear you laugh. You are the only woman who has had a sense of gaiety,
a wise tolerance – no, more, you seem to urge me to betray you. I love
you for that. And what makes you do that – love? Oh it is beautiful to

love and to be free at the same time . . . I love you laughingly . . . Come here quickly and screw me. Shoot with me. Wrap you legs around me. Warm me.' When *Tropic of Cancer* was published in 1934, Miller became famous and notorious for this and his *Rosy Crucifixion* trilogy. Anaïs became famous for her diaries and novels such as *A Spy in the House of Love*. Her erotic short stories *Delta of Venus* changed female eroticism when finally published posthumously in 1977. Their affair ended after ten years but they remained friends for life – and master letter-writers. This letter catches the passion and the hatred of their ménage a trois – and Anaïs's generosity of spirit.

You are right, in one sense, when you speak of honesty. An effort, anyway, with the usual human or feminine retractions. To retreat is not feminine, male, or trickery. It is a terror before utter destruction. What we analyze inexorably, will it die? Will June die? Will our love die, suddenly, instantaneously if you should make a caricature of it? Henry, there is danger in too much knowledge. You have a passion for absolute knowledge. That is why people will hate you.

And sometimes I believe your relentless analysis of June leaves something out, which is your feeling for her beyond knowledge, or in spite of knowledge. I often see how you sob over what you destroy, how you want to stop and just worship; and you do stop, and then a moment later you are at it again with a knife, like a surgeon.

What will you do after you have revealed all there is to know about June? Truth. What ferocity in your quest of it. You destroy and you suffer. In some strange way I am not with you, I am against you. We are destined to hold two truths. I love you and I fight you. And you, the same. We will be stronger for it, each of us, stronger with our love and our hate. When you caricature and nail down and tear apart, I hate you. I want to answer you, not with weak or stupid

poetry but with a wonder as strong as your reality. I want
to fight your surgical knife with all the occult and magical
forces of the world.

I want to both combat you and submit to you, because as
a woman I adore your courage, I adore the pain it engenders,
I adore the struggle you carry in yourself, which I alone
fully realize, I adore your terrifying sincerity. I adore your
strength. You are right. The world is to be caricatured, but
I know, too, how much you can love what you caricature.
How much passion there is in you! It is that I feel in you. I
do not feel the savant, the revealer, the observer. When I am
with you, it is the blood I sense.

This time you are not going to awake from the ecstasies
of our encounters to reveal only the ridiculous moments.
No. You won't do it this time, because while we live
together, while you examine my indelible rouge effacing the
design of my mouth, spreading like blood after an operation
(you kissed my mouth and it was gone, the design of it was
lost as in a watercolor, the colors ran); while you do that, I
seize upon the wonder that is brushing by (the wonder, oh,
the wonder of my lying under you), and I bring it to you,
I breathe it around you. Take it. I feel prodigal with my
feelings when you love me, feelings so unblunted, so new,
Henry, not lost in resemblance to other moments, so much
ours, yours, mine, you and I together, not any man or any
woman together.

What is more touchingly real than your room. The iron
bed, the hard pillow, the single glass. And all sparkling
like a Fourth of July illumination because of my joy, the
soft billowing joy of the womb you inflamed. The room is
full of the incandescence you poured into me. The room
will explode when I sit at the side of your bed and you talk
to me. I don't hear your words: your voice reverberated
against my body like another kind of caress, another kind

of penetration. I have no power over your voice. It comes straight from you to me. I could stuff my ears ad it would find its way into my blood and make it rise.

I am impervious to the flat visual attack of things. I see your khaki shirt hung up on a peg. It is your shirt and I could see you in it – you, wearing a color I detest. But I see you, not the khaki shirt. Something stirs in me as I look at it, and it is certainly the human you. It is a vision of the human you revealing an amazing delicacy to me. It is your khaki shirt and you are the man who is the axis of my world now. I revolve around the richness of your being.

'Come closer to me, come closer. I promise you it will be beautiful.'

You keep your promise.

Listen, I do not believe that I alone feel that we are living something new because it is new to me. I do not see in your writing any of the feelings you have shown me or any of the phrases you have used. When I read your writing, I wondered, What episode are we going to repeat?

You carry your vision, and I mine, and they have mingled. If at moments I see the world as you see it (because they are Henry's whores I love them), you will sometimes see it as I do.

Alexandra to Rasputin, 1909

All of Russia was gripped by the nature of the empress Alexandra's relationship with her confidant, Siberian peasant holy man, Grigory Rasputin. It was a fascination that, step by step, would destroy the monarchy's prestige.

From 1905 when they first meet him, Alexandra, her husband Tsar Nicholas II and their children write regularly to Rasputin who gives them all advice and guidance. The tsarina believes that he has the power to stop the bleeding of her haemophiliac son Alexei. But as this letter shows, Rasputin is also essential to the tsar and tsarina as a combination of priest, psychiatrist and adviser. They revere him as a Christ-like link to God and an authentic peasant who confirms their belief in the mystical connection between tsar and people. It is astonishing that this haughty, neurotic monarch, granddaughter of Queen Victoria, wishes to kiss his hands and sleep next to him but contrary to popular belief, Alexandra was extremely prim: she had no sexual contact with Rasputin. He is, as she writes, 'my beloved mentor'. It is a reverence that endures to his murder in 1916 and beyond, to the murder of the Romanovs themselves in July 1918 when their bodies are still wearing keepsakes given to them by Rasputin.

It was a mark of Rasputin's lack of judgement that he allowed this letter to fall into the hands of a rival priest who deliberately leaked it to embarrass Rasputin and his royal patrons. When it was published, many thought it was too outrageous to be real. But it was genuine.

My beloved and unforgettable teacher, saviour and mentor.

How tiring it is for me to be without you. My soul is calm and I can rest only when you, my teacher, are seated next to me, and I kiss your hands and lay my head on your blessed shoulders. Oh, how easy things are for me then. Then I wish only for one thing – to fall asleep, fall asleep forever on your shoulders, in your embrace. Oh, what happiness it is just to feel your presence near me. Where are you? Whither have you flown? It's so difficult for me, such longing in my heart ... But you, my beloved mentor, don't say a word to Anya [Vyrubova, Alexandra's friend] about my sufferings without you. Anya is good, she is kind, she loves me, but don't tell her of my sorrow. Will you soon be here near me? Come soon. I am waiting for you and am miserable without you. Give me your holy blessing, and I kiss your blessed hands.

Loving you for all times. Mama.

Horatio Nelson to Emma Hamilton, 29 January 1800

Horatio Nelson had first met Emma, Lady Hamilton, beautiful former actress and wife of the super-rich British ambassador to the court of Naples, in the first years of the wars against Revolutionary France. When they met again, Nelson had become Britain's foremost naval hero and a physical wreck. He had already lost an eye ('I got a little hurt his morning'), and had an arm amputated ('the sooner it's off the better') after being wounded in battle. Then in August 1798 he fought the Battle of the Nile – 'Before this time tomorrow, I shall have gained a peerage or Westminster Abbey'. Hit by shot on the forehead with a flap of skin obscuring his remaining eye, he said 'I am killed. Remember me to my wife.' But the wound was light and he wiped out Napoleon Bonaparte's fleet, leaving the French general stranded in Egypt.

Afterwards, he became a legend – Baron Nelson of the Nile and Duke of Bronte – and spent much time being lionised in the exotic city of Naples where he and Emma fell in love. Nelson is forty-two, a ruin of a man, and she is thirty-five and still beautiful. The lovers spend much time with her old husband, the ambassador Sir William Hamilton, a scandal which naturally reaches the ears of Nelson's long-suffering wife Fanny and London society.

When peace was finally signed with France, Nelson and the Hamiltons went on a European cruise during which their daughter Horatia was conceived, returning to London in 1800. Emma was besieged with admirers, including the Prince Regent, and when Nelson grew jealous Hamilton wrote a rather unusual letter to him, insisting that his wife, in her infidelity to himself, was staying faithful to Nelson.

When the war started again in 1804, Nelson moved to confront the Franco-Spanish fleet, first writing a will ordering that Emma be granted 'ample provision to maintain her rank in life', and that his 'adopted daughter, Horatia Nelson Thompson ... use in future the name of Nelson only'. Nelson destroyed the Franco-Spanish fleet at Trafalgar but was shot dead by a French sniper. He was buried in St Paul's Cathedral but his will was ignored: Emma died in penury ten years later.

This blazingly ardent letter, dates from the first days of their passion: ordered to report to his admiral at Livorno, every mile away from Emma is agony. Nelson has promised to not 'sleep on shore' – lest he flirt with anyone else – and swears not even to enjoy pudding, until he makes love to her again. The 'obstacles' are their spouses, Sir William Hamilton and Fanny Nelson.

Separated from all I hold dear in this world what is the use of living if indeed such an existence can be called so, nothing could alleviate such a separation but the call of our Country but loitering time away with nonsense is too much. No separation no time my only beloved Emma can alter my love and affection for you, it is founded on the truest principles of honour, and it only remains for us to regret which I do with the bitterest anguish that there are any obstacles to our being united in the closest ties of this world's rigid rules, as we are in those of real love. Continue only to love your faithful Nelson as he loves his Emma. You are my guide I submit to you, let me find all my fond heart hopes and wishes with the risk of my life. I have been faithful to my word never to partake of any amusement: or to sleep on shore.

Thursday January 30th: we have been six days from Leghorn and no prospect of our making a passage to Palermo, to me it is worse than death. I can neither eat nor sleep for thinking of you my dearest love, I never touch even pudding you know the reason. No I would starve sooner. My only hope is to find you have equally kept your promises to me, for I never made you a promise that I did not as strictly keep as if made in the presence of heaven, but I rest perfectly confident of the reality of your love and that you would die sooner than be false in the smallest thing to your own faithful Nelson who lives only for his Emma.

Friday, I shall run mad we have had a gale of wind that is nothing but I am 20 Leagues farther from you than yesterday noon. Was I master notwithstanding the weather I would have been 20 Leagues nearer but my Commander in Chief knows not what I feel by absence. Last night I did nothing but dream of you altho' I woke 20 times in the night. In one of my dreams I thought I was at a large table. You was not present, sitting between a Princess who I detest and another, they both tried to seduce me and the first wanted to take those liberties with me which no woman in this world but yourself ever did, the consequence was I knocked her down and in the moment of bustle you came in and taking me in your embrace whispered I love nothing but you my Nelson. I kissed you fervently and we enjoy'd the height of love. Ah Emma I pour out my soul to you. If you love any thing but me you love those who feel not like your N.

Sunday noon, fair Wind which makes me a little better in hopes of seeing you my love my Emma is tomorrow, just 138 miles distant, and I trust to find you like myself, for no love is like mine towards you.

Napoleon Bonaparte to Josephine, 24 April 1796

Theirs is a love match. He is the young victorious general of Revolutionary France; she is a Creole girl born in Martinique, the widow of an aristocrat guillotined during the Terror of the early 1790s. She became the mistress of Paul Barras, one of the ruling Directors of France who then introduced her to his rising general Napoleon, whom she married on 9 March 1796. Afterwards, Napoleon defeated France's enemies – the Austrians, the Russians, the Prussians, the Egyptians and himself seized power in France. In 1804, he crowned himself and Josephine emperor and empress. But he needed an heir and the marriage had produced no children. He therefore divorced Josephine and married Archduchess Marie Louise, Habsburg daughter of the Emperor of Austria, with whom he had a son. When Napoleon lost his empire and went into exile in 1814, Josephine was admired by all for enduring all these blows with her characteristic style – but she died just months later.

This letter finds her in Paris while General Bonaparte is fighting in Italy – just after their marriage, but already he is craving her, tormented with jealousy. She is fashionable and chic, flirtatious and unfaithful, he is obsessional, controlling and puppyishly devoted, bombarding her with letters that praise, seduce, threaten, whine and boast in equal parts. He raves about her body and her sexual technique, something called the 'zigzag', begging her not to wash so he could smell her. As we read in this letter, he always wants to kiss her on the heart as well as 'lower down, much lower'.

My brother will bring you this letter. I have the greatest love for him and I hope he will gain yours; he deserves it. Nature has given him a sweet and utterly good character; he is full of good qualities.

I am writing to Barras to get him appointed consul in some Italian port. He wants to live with his little wife far away from the hurly-burly and political affairs; I commend him to you.

I have your letters of the 16th and the 21st. There are many days when you don't write. What do you do, then?

No, my darling, I am not jealous, but sometimes worried.

Come soon; I warn you, if you delay, you will find me ill. Fatigue and your absence are too much.

Your letters are the joy of my days, and my days of happiness are not many.

Junot is bringing twenty-two flags to Paris. You must come back with him, do you understand?

Hopeless sorrow, inconsolable misery, sadness without end, if I am so unhappy as to see him return alone.

Adorable friend, he will see you, he will breathe in your temple; perhaps you will grant him the unique and perfect flavor of kissing your cheek, and I shall be alone and far, far away.

But you are coming, aren't you? You are going to be here beside me, in my arms, on my breast, on my mouth.

Take wing and come, come! But travel gently. The road is long, bad, tiring.

Suppose you had an accident, or fell ill; suppose fatigue – come gently, my adorable love, but I think of you often.

I have received a letter from Hortense [Josephine's daughter who would marry Napoleon's brother Louis, future king of Holland]. I will write to her. She is altogether charming. I love her and will soon send her the perfumes she wants.

Read Ossian's poem 'Carthon' carefully, and sleep well and happily far from your good friend, but thinking of him.

A kiss on the heart, and one lower down, much lower!

B.

I don't know if you need money; you have never talked about your business matters. If so, you can ask my brother, who has 200 louis of mine.

Alexander II to Katya Dolgorukaya, January 1868

Alexander II's correspondence with Katya is probably the most explicit ever written by a political leader. But the letters are also poignant, passionate and political. He is aged around forty, the most attractive of the Romanov emperors – a reformer who has just liberated the serfs – when he falls in love with a teenage girl about to leave school: Princess Ekaterina Dolgorukaya. One day in January 1865 they bump into each other in the park outside her boarding school minutes before a terrorist tries to assassinate the tsar. Alexander regards their love as sacredly sanctioned, her as a guardian angel. Bored with his prim wife and heartbroken after the death of his eldest son, Alexander finds himself under astonishing pressure as terrorists launch an assassination campaign against him. His consolation is Katya, with whom he shares the comfort of love and a mutually intense eroticism. In several letters a day, scrawled in French, they relish their sexual sessions together using the code word *bingerle* for sex.

In their letters, Alexander remembers the first time they met in secret: 'I'll never forget what happened on the sofa in the mirrored room when we kissed on the mouth for the first time, and you made me go out while you removed your crinoline which was in our way and I was surprised to find you without your pantaloons. Oh, oh *quelle horreur*? I was almost mad at this dream but it was real and I felt HE was bursting. I felt a frenzy. That's when I encountered my treasure . . . I would have given anything to dip inside again . . . I was electrified that your saucy crinoline let me touch your legs that only I had ever seen . . . We fell on each other like wild cats . . .' She is just as enthusiastic, writing: 'You know I want you. I received immense pleasure and feel overwhelmed by it, pleasure incomparable to everything else', and he often replies: 'compliments from mon *bingerle* which is fully armed'. But they also discuss politics and war and share the happiness of their growing family of children.

When Alexander's wife died in 1880, he married Katya, now Princess Yurovskaya, but in 1881, terrorists assassinated Alexander. Katya retired to Paris. Here's one of the *bingerle* letters from early in their relationship:

At ten in the morning.
  Bonjour my angel, I love you more than life and
am happy to love you, my heart belongs to you totally

forever. . . I await your letter with a feverish impatience and can't understand what delays it.

At four in the afternoon.

I want you more madly than ever my adored angel . . . The ceremony went well but I swear I am still exhausted from our delicious *bingerles* and the exertions of this morning, but we could once again experience the happiness that we know together, I would certainly not rush and never interrupt our *bingerle*. Yes certainly I feel that I have become your life and I'd only like it that you don't forget that you are mine and I've only everywhere one idea in my head – it's you my angel, joy, happiness, consolation, courage, my everything. Nothing else exists for me. Thank you for telling me that your life has become something thanks to me. You couldn't give me a greater pleasure because that tells me that you feel loved and you understand what you've become for me. Without you, my existence would be impossible and I would follow you in into the tomb. May God pity us and give us one day the possibility of only living for us. There couldn't be a couple more loving. Thanks to our delicious evening and our encounter of the morning, I feel totally impregnated with the brilliant and joyous moments that come to me without ceasing. I see myself in my imagination lying in the arms of my adorable pixie and adoring your [illegible word] that I adore like all the rest of your darling being and I can't forget the expression in your adorable eyes during our *bingerles* which reflects the pleasure that you give and that you share with the very being, body and soul, more than ever. How can I not be mad for you after that, my angel, my everything? So tomorrow we have the chance to see each other in the morning during my promenade and the evening at the wedding where our looks will express what we feel. Monday morning you tell what you can do and in the evening I hope to meet to complete our interrupted *bingerle* . . . I want you to know that you delight my being, which belongs to you for ever, it's love for you more than ever. I would like to eat you, kiss you taste you . . .

Josef Stalin to Pelageya Onufrieva, 29 February 1912

The pleasure of private letters is that they sometimes reveal lost aspects of familiar characters. Here in 1912, Josef Djugashvili, a Bolshevik revolutionary of Georgian origins who later adopts the name 'Stalin', writes a love letter of passionate 'kiiissssing' to his schoolgirl mistress Pelageya. They have met in Vologda where Stalin is in exile and she is the mistress of one of Stalin's friends. She is around sixteen, he is thirty-four. He lectures her about Shakespeare, art and philosophy. He calls her 'Hot Polya' and she calls him 'Oddball Osip' – a diminutive for Josef. She knows that when he leaves they would never meet again. As the future tyrant of the Soviet Union catches a late train to Moscow, to vanish again and return to his work in the revolutionary underworld, he buys a postcard of Rodin's sculpture The Kiss – a couple kissing –and sends this to Polya.

Dear PG,

I got your letter today . . . Don't write to the old address since none of us are there any more . . . I owe you a kiss for the kiss, passed on to me by Peter. Let me kiss you now. I'm not simply sending a kiss but am kiiissssing you passionately (it's not worth kissing any other way),

Josef

Family

Elizabeth I to Mary I, 16 March 1554

This is the letter that saves a princess. It is the reign of Queen Mary, daughter of Henry VIII and Queen Catherine of Aragon – a dangerous time for her semi-legitimate half-sister Elizabeth, daughter of Henry VIII and his short-lived queen, Anne Boleyn, executed as an adulteress and regarded by Mary as a whorish Protestant heretic.

In 1553 when Henry's successor Edward VI died young, powerful factions tried to impose a Protestant monarch with a tenuous claim, Lady Jane Grey. But Mary was a king's daughter, even if she was a Catholic one, and she was accepted as rightful queen. Once she started to reimpose Catholicism and agreed to marry the Catholic King Philip of Spain, she faced a rebellion led by Thomas Wyatt, who planned to replace her with Elizabeth. To force him to implicate Elizabeth, Wyatt was tortured. He was then executed.

Elizabeth is arrested, but the intelligent and vigilant twenty-one-year-old shrewdly appeals direct to her sister. As she is about to be transferred to the sinister and looming Tower of London, where princes and princesses of royal blood have been executed or murdered, she writes this letter. She cites the recent case of the duke of Somerset, Lord Protector under the young Edward VI, who allowed the execution of his own brother Lord Admiral Thomas Seymour for conspiracy – and for trying to marry Elizabeth herself. It is known as the 'Tide Letter' because Elizabeth deliberately writes it so slowly that the tide has turned before it is finished, delaying her remand to the Tower for a day. In its well-chosen words, we can hear one of Henry VIII's daughters begging for her life from another. Elizabeth was later taken to the Tower, but then released. On Mary's death, she succeeded to the throne, becoming perhaps England's greatest monarch. Her survival would confirm the independent and Protestant path of English history.

If any ever did try this old saying, 'that a king's word was more than another man's oath,' I most humbly beseech

your Majesty to verify it to me, and to remember your last
promise and my last demand, that I be not condemned
without answer and due proof, which it seems that I now
am; for without cause proved, I am by your council from
you commanded to go to the Tower, a place more wanted
for a false traitor than a true subject, which though I know
I desire it not, yet in the face of all this realm it appears
proved. I pray to God I may die the shamefullest death
that any ever died, if I may mean any such thing; and to
this present hour I protest before God (Who shall judge
my truth, whatsoever malice shall devise), that I never
practised, counselled, nor consented to anything that might
be prejudicial to your person anyway, or dangerous to the
state by any means. And therefore I humbly beseech your
Majesty to let me answer afore yourself, and not suffer
me to trust to your Councillors, yea, and that afore I go
to the Tower, if it be possible; if not, before I be further
condemned. Howbeit, I trust assuredly your Highness will
give me leave to do it afore I go, that thus shamefully I may
not be cried out on, as I now shall be; yea, and that without
cause. Let conscience move your Highness to pardon this
my boldness, which innocency procures me to do, together
with hope of your natural kindness, which I trust will not
see me cast away without desert, which what it is I would
desire no more of God but that you truly knew, but which
thing I think and believe you shall never by report know,
unless by yourself you hear. I have heard of many in my
time cast away for want of coming to the presence of their
Prince; and in late days I heard my Lord of Somerset say that
if his brother had been suffered to speak with him he had
never suffered; but persuasions were made to him so great
that he was brought in belief that he could not live safely
if the Admiral lived, and that made him give consent to his
death. Though these persons are not to be compared to your

Majesty, yet I pray to God the like evil persuasions persuade not one sister against the other, and all for that they have heard false report, and the truth not known. Therefore, once again, kneeling with humbleness of heart, because I am not suffered to bow the knees of my body, I humbly crave to speak with your Highness, which I would not be so bold as to desire if I knew not myself most clear, as I know myself most true. And as for the traitor Wyatt, he might peradventure write me a letter, but on my faith I never received any from him. And as for the copy of the letter sent to the French King, I pray God confound me eternally if ever I sent him word, message, token, or letter, by any means, and to this truth I will stand in till my death.

   Your Highness's most faithful subject, that hath been from the beginning, and will be to my end,
   ELIZABETH

I humbly crave but only one word of answer from yourself.

Vilma Grünwald to Kurt Grünwald, 11 July 1944

Few letters survive from the death camps built by the Nazis to exterminate the Jewish people during the Holocaust. Here is an almost unreadably poignant short note, from the Czech prisoner Vilma Grünwald to her doctor husband Kurt. She, Kurt and their two children, John and Frank (Misa), were arrested like thousands of other innocent Jewish families and transported to Auschwitz. At the selection, the SS doctor Josef Mengele sends the limping John to the left – for instant execution in the extermination camp. His mother, knowing what this means, chooses to join him in an act of maternal love. She writes this note moments after she and John have been separated from the other two, then hands it to a guard and asks him to convey it to Kurt, who would be set to work in the neighbouring slave labour camp as a physician responsible for restoring injured prisoners to a state that they might work again. Vilma and John are gassed moments later.

Amazingly, the letter reached Kurt, who survived the Holocaust, and upon his release was reunited with his surviving son Frank, who eventually donated the letter to the United States Holocaust Memorial Museum.

You, my only one, dearest, in isolation we are waiting for darkness. We considered the possibility of hiding but decided not to do it since we felt it would be hopeless. The famous trucks are already here and we are waiting for it to begin. I am completely calm. You – my only and dearest one, do not blame yourself for what happened, it was our destiny. We did what we could. Stay healthy and remember my words that time will heal – if not completely – then – at least partially. Take care of the little golden boy and don't spoil him too much with your love. Both of you – stay healthy, my dear ones. I will be thinking of you and Misa. Have a fabulous life, we must board the trucks.

Into eternity, Vilma.

Kadashman-Enlil to Amenhotep III, c.1370 BC

Fathers often take a view about who their daughters should marry, and that has not changed over the three millennia since this letter was written. It is from one king to another, and royal daughters have often been treated as political pawns by their fathers.

The Babylonian king Kadashman-Enlil was a contemporary of the Egyptian pharaoh Amenhotep III the Magnificent, and the two were frequent correspondents.

This is one of the Amarna letters, carved on clay tablets, that were discovered in 1887 in the new sacred capital Akhenaten (today el-Amarna), founded by Amenhotep's son Pharaoh Akhenaten. These diplomatic letters, 382 of them, written in Akkadian cuneiform, were probably stored in the Bureau of the Pharaoh's Correspondence, and may well be the most revealing letters of the early ancient world.

Here, Kadashman-Enlil smarts at the insult of being refused one of Amenhotep's daughters, before offering one of his own daughters in return for gold. Egyptian monarchs regarded themselves as far too important to give their daughters to foreign rulers – but the Babylonian is clearly irritated by this pharoanic arrogance, an irritation that may only be soothed with gold, gold and more gold . . .

How is it possible that, having written to you in order to ask for the hand of your daughter – oh my brother, you should have written me using such language, telling me that you will not give her to me as since earliest times no daughter of the king of Egypt has ever been given in marriage? Why are you telling me such things? You are the king. You may do as you wish. If you wanted to give me your daughter in marriage who could say you nay?

But you, keeping to your principle of not sending anybody, have not sent me a wife. Have you not been looking for a fraternal and amical relationship, when you suggested to me – in writing – a marriage, in order to make us become closer? Why hasn't my brother sent me a wife? . . . It is possible for you not to send me a wife, but how could I refuse you a wife and not send her to you, as you did? I have daughters, I will not refuse you in any way concerning this . . .

As to the gold about which I wrote you, send me now quickly during this summer . . . before your messenger reaches me, gold in abundance, as much as is available. I could thus achieve the task I have undertaken. If you send me this summer . . . the gold concerning which I've written to you, I shall give you my daughter in marriage. Therefore, send gold, willingly, as much as you please. But if you do not send me gold . . . so I can achieve the task I have undertaken, why haven't you sent me any earlier willingly? After I have finished the task I have undertaken, why would I wish for gold? Even if you sent me 3000 talents of gold I would not accept them. I would return them and would not give you my daughter in marriage.

Oliver Cromwell to Valentine Walton, 4 July 1644

Even victory has its heartbreaks. Two days after his defeat of the forces of Charles I at Marston Moor, one of the bloodiest battles of the English Civil War and the largest ever fought on English soil, Oliver Cromwell writes to his brother-in-law. He celebrates the victory as a 'great favour from the Lord' for his side, 'the Godly Party', but also has to inform Walton that his son, young Valentine, has been killed in the battle. This is a classic letter of English history: as the Parliamentarian cavalry commander, Cromwell is the military genius who has created the Ironside cavalry that will decisively contribute to victory over the king.

Born in 1599 in Huntingdon, Cromwell was an obscure provincial gentleman until elected to Parliament at the height of its crisis with King Charles. Having no military experience, he recruited his own troop, ultimately commanding the New Model Army. Ruthless and fanatically religious, known as 'Old Ironside', this psalm-singing general emerged from the Civil War as the dominant Parliamentary leader, reluctantly overseeing the execution of the king. In the new republic known as the 'Commonwealth' he defeated all challengers, including the Scots, and led an invasion of Ireland, during which he suppressed the Catholics in a series of massacres. In 1653 he was elected as a quasi-king as Lord Protector. This letter shows his sanctimony and harshness – it is hard to forget the image of mowing down the royal cavalry like 'stubble to our swords' but, having lost children himself, Cromwell also shows his softer side.

To my loving Brother,

    Colonel Valentine Walton: These

It's our duty to sympathize in all mercies; and to praise the Lord together in chastisements or trials, that so we may sorrow together.

Truly England and the Church of God hath had a great favour from the Lord, in this great victory given unto us, such as the like never was since this war began.

It had all the evidences of an absolute victory obtained by the Lord's blessing upon the Godly Party principally. We never charged but we routed the enemy. The Left Wing, which I commanded, being our own horse, saving a few Scots in our rear, beat all the Prince's horse. God made them as stubble to our swords. We charged their regiments of foot with our horse, and routed all we charged. The particulars I cannot relate now; but I believe, of twenty thousand the Prince hath not four thousand left. Give glory, all the glory, to God.

Sir, God hath taken away your eldest son by a cannon-shot. It brake his leg. We were necessitated to have it cut off, whereof he died.

Sir, you know my own trials this way: but the Lord supported me with this, That the Lord took him into the happiness we all pant for and live for. There is your precious child full of glory, never to know sin or sorrow any more. He was a gallant young man, exceedingly gracious. God give you His comfort. Before his death he was so full of comfort that to Frank Russel and myself he could not express it, 'It was so great above his pain.' This he said to us. Indeed it was admirable. A little after, he said, One thing lay upon his spirit. I asked him, What that was? he told me it was, That God had not suffered him to be any more the executioner of His enemies. At his fall, his horse being killed with the bullet, and as I am informed three horses more, I am told he bid them, Open to the right and left, that he might see the rogues run. Truly he was exceedingly beloved in the Army, of all that knew him. But few knew him; for he was a precious young man, fit for God. You have cause to bless the Lord. He is a glorious Saint in Heaven; wherein you ought exceedingly to rejoice. Let this drink up your sorrow; seeing these are not feigned words to comfort you, but the thing is real and undoubted a truth. You may do all things by the strength of Christ. Seek that, and you shall easily bear your trial. Let this public mercy to the Church of God make you to forget your private sorrow. The Lord be your strength: so prays

Your truly faithful and loving brother,
OLIVER CROMWELL

Toussaint L'Ouverture to Napoleon, 12 July 1802

'I was born a slave but nature gave me the soul of a free man.' François-Dominique Toussaint was a black slave on the French colony Sainte-Domingue on the island of Hispaniola. Intelligent, gifted and educated, he was freed from slavery and then managed a French plantation as well as somehow picking up a mix of Western and Creole medical knowledge, ultimately running his own estate with his own slaves. But in 1791, the French Revolution inspired a rebellion by the slaves of the island and he soon emerged as their leader. By 1793, he had earned the nickname L'Ouverture, 'The Opener', in battle, and made this declaration: 'Brothers and friends, I am Toussaint L'Ouverture; perhaps my name has made itself known to you. I have undertaken vengeance. I want Liberty and Equality to reign in St Domingue. I am working to make that happen. Unite yourselves to us, brothers, and fight with us for the same cause.'

Fighting first with the Spanish against the French, then vice versa, then against the French again, L'Ouverture became Governor-General, autocrat for life of the first black republic, issuing a constitution while remaining formally under France. Napoleon Bonaparte, First Consul of France, sent an army. L'Ouverture ordered his commander Dessalines to burn Port-au-Prince: 'Set that place on fire ... Don't forget we have no other resource than destruction and flames ... Tear up the roads with shot; throw corpses and horses into all the fountains; burn and annihilate everything in order that those who've come to reduce us to slavery may before their eyes have the image of hell they deserve.' But Toussaint was tricked and captured. His wife Suzanne and family were arrested. Here, held on a French warship, the broken Toussaint writes this pitiful letter begging for the freedom of his family. Shipped to France, he died in prison but within a year, the French were defeated and his creation, Haiti, achieved independence.

CITIZEN FIRST CONSUL: I will not conceal my faults from you. I have committed some. What man is exempt? I am quite ready to avow them. After the word of honuor of the Captain-General who represents the French Government, after a proclamation addressed to the colony, in which he promised to throw the veil of oblivion over the events which had taken place in Saint Domingo, I, as you did on the 18th Brumaire, withdrew into the bosom of my family. Scarcely had a month passed away, when evil-disposed persons, by means of intrigues, effected my ruin with the General-in-chief, by filling his mind with distrust against me. I received a letter from him which ordered me to act in conjunction with General Brunet. I obeyed. Accompanied by two persons, I went to Gonaïves, where I was arrested. They sent me on board the frigate Creole, I know not for what reason, without any other clothes than those I had on. The next day my house was exposed to pillage; my wife and my children were arrested; they had nothing, not even the means to cover themselves.

Citizen First Consul: A mother fifty years of age may deserve the indulgence and the kindness of a generous and liberal nation. She has no account to render. I alone ought to be responsible for my conduct to the Government I have served. I have too high an idea of the greatness and the justice of the First Magistrate of the French people, to doubt a moment of its impartiality. I indulge the feeling that the balance in its hands will not incline to one side more than to another. I claim its generosity.

Salutations and respect,

Toussaint Louverture

Alexander I to his sister Catherine, 20 September 1805

This letter shows how royal families are different from the rest of us. Tsar Alexander I was tall, blonde, handsome and all-powerful, but he was also flawed: he colluded in the murder of his own father, a crime he never recovered from. His greatest love was 'Catiche', the little sister who was so much younger that he treated her more like a girlfriend than a sibling. In 1805, as Alexander confronts Napoleon for the first time, he writes her what amount to half love letters, saying he wants to kiss the nose and feet of 'the Little Mad Thing'. But in some ways, Catiche was tougher than Alexander. A few weeks after this, he was catastrophically defeated by Napoleon.

Absurd Little Mad Thing,

Get out of your head that to answer you is a trouble to me. As soon as I have a moment it is a real pleasure, for I love few things in the world like my Bisiam.

The news you gave me of Aunt was a real pleasure to me, if she is kind enough to think of me. I assure you no day goes by without my thinking of her. Tell her so, I beg of you, from me. Farewell, light of my eyes, adored of my heart, polestar of the age, wonder of Nature, or better than all these, Bisiam Bisiamovna with the snub nose.

There is a lot left of the white grease which they put on the wheels. I should like to send you some to keep up that kind of softness in the muscles of the nose on which I press the tenderest of kisses.

All yours, heart and soul, Alexander.

Charles I to Charles II, 29 November 1648

Charles I succeeded his father James I in 1625. Determined to rule without the restraints of an overmighty Parliament, Charles was successful in this respect until multiple crises forced him to call a new Parliament in 1640. The confrontation between king and Parliament, exacerbated by religious conflicts, led to a civil war which Charles ultimately lost. Here, in late 1648, as Oliver Cromwell and his New Model Army consolidate control of the kingdom, Charles I is being held by Parliamentary forces in Newport where, after a failed attempt to escape to the continent, he is engaged in fruitless negotiations to save both his throne and life.

Charles knows that many on the Parliamentary side now regard him as a feckless 'Man of Blood' who can no longer be trusted, and support a republic. Even the unthinkable is now possible: the trial and execution of a divinely sanctioned monarch. Most of the royal family including his beloved wife Henrietta Maria have escaped to the continent. Their eldest son Charles, Prince of Wales, is in the Hague. The king writes to his son, knowing he may never see him again. It is a letter on kingship – but also on how to behave and how to live – from a doomed father to a faraway son.

In January 1649 the king was tried, sentenced to death and beheaded. England became a republic and protectorate until 1660, when the son acceded to the throne as Charles II.

Newport, November 29, 1648

Son,

By what hath been said, you may see how long we have laboured in search of peace. Do not you be discouraged to tread these ways, to restore yourself to your right; but prefer the way of peace. Show the greatness of your mind, rather to conquer your enemies by pardoning than punishing. If you saw how unmanly and unchristianly this implacable disposition is in our evil willers, you would avoid that spirit. Censure us not, for having parted with too much of our own right; the price was great; the commodity was security to us, peace to our people. And we are confident another Parliament would remember how useful a King's power is to a people's liberty.

Of how much have we divested ourself, that we and they might meet again in a due Parliamentary way to agree the bounds for Prince and people! And in this, give belief to our experience, never to affect more greatness or prerogative than what is really and intrinsically for the good of our subjects (not satisfaction of favourites). And if you thus use it, you will never want means to be a father to all, and a bountiful Prince to any you would be extraordinarily gracious to. You may perceive all men trust their treasure, where it returns them interest: and if Princes, like the sea, receive and repay all the fresh streams and rivers trust them with, they will not grudge, but pride themselves, to make them up an ocean.

These considerations may make you a great Prince, as your father is now a low one; and your state may be so much the more established, as mine hath been shaken. For subjects have learnt (we dare say) that victories over their Princes are but triumphs over themselves; and so, will be more unwilling to hearken to changes hereafter.

The English nation are a sober people; however at present

under some infatuation. We know not but this may be the last time we may speak to you or the world publicly. We are sensible into what hands we are fallen; and yet we bless God we have those inward refreshments, that the malice of our enemies cannot disturb. We have learnt to own ourself by retiring into ourself, and therefore can the better digest what befalls us; not doubting but God can restrain our enemies' malice, and turn their fierceness unto his praise.

To conclude, if God give you success, use it humbly and far from revenge. If He restore you to your right upon hard conditions, whatever you promise, keep. Those men which have forced laws which they were bound to observe, will find their triumphs full of troubles. Do not think anything in this world worth obtaining by foul and unjust means. You are the son of our love; and, as we direct you to what we have recommended to you, so we assure you, we do not more affectionately pray for you (to whom we are a natural parent) than we do, that the ancient glory and renown of this nation be not buried in irreligion and fanatic humour: and that all our subjects (to whom we are a political parent) may have such sober thoughts as to seek their peace in the orthodox profession of the Christian religion, as it was established since the Reformation in this kingdom, and not in new revelation; and that the ancient laws, with the interpretation according to the known practices, may once again be a hedge about them; that you may in due time govern, and they be governed, as in the fear of the Lord.

C.R

Svetlana Stalina to her father Stalin, mid 1930s

What happens when your children decide to play dictator for a day? Growing up in the Kremlin, Svetlana, the daughter of the Soviet dictator Josef Stalin, likes to play this game. From the age of seven to eleven, she often writes orders that every child in the world would love to put into effect. One day, she orders her 'First Secretary' (Stalin) and other 'Secretaries' (of the Communist Party) that all homework be cancelled in all Soviet schools. Stalin enormously enjoyed playing the game and signed all her orders, as did the rest of the Politburo. They were then pinned up on the board in the Stalin kitchen. Stalin called her 'Svetlana the Boss' or 'Setanka, Mistress of the House', and usually answered: 'I obey. Setanka's little secretary. Stalin.' Svetlana signed herself 'First Secretary of the Communist Party' or 'Boss'. In this 'order', she demands to know what is really happening in the very secretive ruling Central Committee through which her father terrorised the Soviet people. Sometimes Stalin requested more orders: 'write to me more often: your Little Secretary [Stalin] will soon not know what to do if he doesn't receive your daily orders and commands.'.

Daily Order No. 3. I order you to show me what happens in the Central Committee! Strictly confidential. Stalina, the Boss.

Augustus to Caius Caesar, 23 September AD 2

An elderly father writes to his son; an ageing emperor writes to his adopted heir. Caesar Augustus (formerly Octavian) has ruled Rome since the assassination of his great-uncle Julius Caesar in 44 BC, and the entire empire as its first emperor since 31. Having no sons of his own, he has adopted his nephews Caius and Lucius to succeed him at his 'sentry post'. Sending Caius on an inspection trip of the Roman provinces he finds that on his sixty-fourth birthday he is missing the 'dearest little donkey'. Sadly, both boys were to die before Augustus himself.

Greetings my dear Caius my dearest little donkey whom, so help me, I constantly miss whenever you are away from me. But especially on such days as today my eyes are eager for my Caius and wherever you have been today I hope you have celebrated my sixty-fourth birthday in health and happiness . . . and I pray the gods that whatever time is left for me I may pass with you safe and well with our country in a flourishing condition while you both are playing the man and preparing to succeed to my sentry post.

Joseph II to his brother Leopold II, 4 October 1777

It was the royal wedding of its time – but seven years into the marriage, something is wrong, and this letter reveals what that is and how to solve it.

In 1770, when she was just fifteen, the Habsburg archduchess of Austria, Marie Antoinette married the Bourbon heir to the French throne, soon to be Louis XVI. She was pretty and playful but also silly, extravagant and unwise. This promised to be a bad combination in an overstretched kingdom on the verge of bankruptcy, which could ill afford any loss of royal prestige. King Louis, for his part, was cloddish, ineffectual and dull. For seven years, while Marie flirted with admirers, Louis struggled to consummate the marriage.

Finally her brother, Emperor Joseph II, comes to visit to see if he can help. In an early example of marriage counselling, Joseph interviews Louis and his sister like an imperial sex therapist. 'What a pair of blunderers,' he writes afterwards in this astonishing letter to his brother, the future Emperor Leopold, concluding that the real problem is not a physical or medical one but merely the queen's lack of interest and the king's laziness. In August, the grateful couple consummated their marriage, and she was soon pregnant with the first of several children.

In 1789, Louis and Marie Antoinette were overthrown and, in 1793, guillotined.

Imagine! In his marriage bed – this is the secret – he has

strong, perfectly satisfactory erections. He introduces the member, stays there for perhaps two minutes without moving, withdraws without ever discharging but still erect, and bids good night. It's incredible, because in addition he sometimes has night-time emissions, but in his bed, never when on the job, and he's happy, saying simply that he only does it out of duty and gets no pleasure from it. Ah! If I could have been present once, I should have arranged it properly. He needs to be whipped, to make him discharge in a passion, like donkeys. Further, my sister is pretty placid, and they're two incompetents together.

Rameses the Great to Hattusili, King of the Hittites, 1243 BC

The arrogance of empire in a letter three thousand years old. Rameses the Great ruled Egypt at its zenith, its master for around fifty years. Earlier in his reign he had fought against the Hittite king Hattusili, but in 1258 BC, following the Battle of Kadesh, they became allies and Rameses deigned to marry a Hittite princess. Here, taking advantage of their good relations, Hattusili asks Rameses if he can help with a sensitive family problem: his sister Matanazi, married to a nearby king, wants to have children even though she is no longer young, and the Hittite asks if Rameses can send priests and healers to make this happen. Here is the Great King's patronising and ungracious answer, sneering that not even Egyptian magic could make a woman of sixty produce children . . .

Thus to my Brother: (Concerning) what my Brother has written to me regarding his sister Matanazi: 'May my Brother send to me a man to prepare medicines so that she may bear children.' So has my Brother written. And so (I say) to my Brother: 'Look, Matanazi, the sister of my

Brother, the king your Brother knows her. She is said to be 50 or even 60 years old! Look, a woman of 50 is old, to say nothing of a 60-year-old! One can't produce medicines to enable her to bear children! Well, the Sun God and the Storm God may give a command, and the order which they give will then be carried out continually for the sister of my Brother. And I, the king your Brother, will send an expert incantation-priest and an expert doctor and they will prepare medicines to assist her to produce children.

Creation

Michelangelo to Giovanni da Pistoia, 1509

Michelangelo Buonarroti was not only a sculptor and artist but also a brilliant poet and superb letter-writer. Sometimes he sent his poems as letters – this is one of the best. He had been hired by the warrior-pope Julius II in 1508 to supervise the painting of the ceiling of the Sistine Chapel in Rome: a somewhat unorthodox choice, given that he was better known as a sculptor at the time.

Julius let Michelangelo 'do as I liked' – nine main scenes that would represent God's creation of the world and of man in Genesis. The work, which would take him until 1512, would be his most timeless achievement. Not only was his vision astonishingly ambitious but the physical strain of actually painting the ceiling was punishing. He had to build his own scaffolding and hang upside down high above the chapel for hours on end, year after year. At one point he writes to his father: 'I lead a miserable existence . . . not of life nor honour . . . I live wearied by stupendous labours and beset by a thousand anxieties . . . never an hour's happiness have I had.' Out of these agonies emerge one of the greatest works of art in the human story. A year into the work's creation, he sends this despairing verse letter to his friend Giovanni da Pistoia, detailing some of the torments that he faced.

'When the Author was Painting the Vault of the Sistine Chapel'
I've already grown a goiter from this torture,
swollen up here like a cat from Lombardy
(or anywhere where the stagnant water's poison).
My stomach's squashed under my chin, my beard's
pointing at heaven, my brain's crushed in a casket,
my breast twists like a harpy's. My brush,
above me all the time, dribbles the paint
so my face makes a fine floor for droppings!

My haunches are grinding into my guts,
my poor ass strains to work as a counterweight,
every gesture I make is blind and aimless.
My skin hangs loose below me, my spine's
all knotted from folding over itself,
I'm bent taut as a Syrian bow.

And because I'm like this, my thoughts
Are crazy perfidious tripe:
Anyone shoots badly through a crooked blowpipe.

My painting is dead.
Defend it for me, Giovanni, protect my honor.
I am not in the right place—I am not a painter.

Wolfgang Amadeus Mozart to his cousin Marianne, 13 November 1777

A letter of manic and scatological exuberance from a musical genius. Brought up in Salzburg and taught music by his ambitious choirmaster father, the young Mozart toured Europe for ten years as a performing pianist and violinist. During the stress of endless touring when he was in his twenties, Mozart enjoyed a madcap friendship and probably passionate relationship with Marianne, – much to his father's disapproval. Their sexual collusion and relish in faecal humour is only too clear in their earthily hilarious letters: 'I shall greet you high and nobly with pizazz,' writes Mozart to the little cousin he called 'Basle', 'and put my personal seal on your ass, I will kiss your hands and have such fun shooting off my rear-end gun, I shall embrace you with a smack and wash you down front and back, I shall pay all I owed you from the start and then let go a resounding fart and perhaps even drop something hard – well adieu my Angel my heart I'm waiting for you PS Shit-dibitare, shit-dibatate, the pastor of Rodempl, he licked the ass of his kitchen maid, to set a good example.'

The child prodigy was first employed by the Prince-Bishop of Salzburg. Then in 1781, determined to make his name, he arrived in Vienna. He thrived creatively in the musical capital of Europe, where he composed his greatest operas and symphonies. But he was only moderately appreciated by Emperor Joseph II, who finally appointed him to the rank of chamber composer. In 1782 Mozart married Constance Weber whom he adored: they had six children. His letters to her are boyishly affectionate: 'I get all excited like a child when I think about being with you again – If people could see into my heart I should almost feel ashamed. Everything is cold to me – ice-cold. – If you were here with me, maybe I would find the courtesies people are showing me more enjoyable – but as it is, it's all so empty – adieu – my dear – I am Forever, your Mozart who loves you with his entire soul. PS. – while I was writing the last page, tear after tear fell on the paper. But I must cheer up – catch – An astonishing number of kisses are flying about – The deuce! – I see a whole crowd of them. Ha! Ha! . . . I have just caught three – They are delicious . . . I kiss you millions of times.'

But nothing quite approaches the outrageous humour of the 'Basle letters', those earlier Mozartian creations, with their anarchic stream of puns, alliteration, songs, echoes and repetitions. They are best read very fast. This one begins with an instruction from his mother to write a 'sensible letter'. But that resolution did not last long . . .

. . . now write her a sensible letter for once, you can still write all that funny stuff, but be sure to tell her that you have received all the mail, so she won't be concerned about it, and worry.

Ma très chère Nièce! Cousine! fille!
Mère, Sœur, et Épouse!

Heaven, Hell, and a thousand sacristies, Croatians, damnations, devils, and witchies, druids, cross-Battalions with no ends, by all the elements, air, water, earth, and fire, Europe, asia, affrica, and America, jesuits, Augustins, Benedictins, Capucins, Minorites, Franciscans, Dominicans, Carthusians, and dignified Holy-Crucians, Canons regular and irregular, and all hairy brutes and snitches, higgledy-piggledy castrates and bitches, asses, buffaloes, oxen, fools, nitwits, and fops! What sort of manner is this, my dear? 4 soldiers and only 3 gear? – such a Paquet no Portrait? – I was already filled with high expectations – I thought for sure – for you wrote it to me yourself not long ago that I would receive it soon, very soon. Are you perhaps doubting whether I will keep my word? – I certainly hope that you have no doubts! Well then, I beg you, do send it to me, the sooner, the better. And I hope it will portray you the way I requested, I mean in french fashion.

How I like Mannheim? – as well as one can like any place without Bääsle. Pardon my poor handwriting, the pen is already old; now I have been shitting for nearly 22 years out of the same old hole and yet it's not torn a whit! – although I used it so often to shit – and then chewed off the muck bit by bit.

I hope, on the other hand, that you have been receiving my letters, as it so happens, one from Hohenaltheim, 2 from Mannheim, and now this one. As it so happens, this one is the third from Mannheim, but all in all it's the 4th, as it so happens. Now I must close, as it so happens, because I am not dressed yet, and we'll be eating soon so that afterward we can go and shit again, as it so happens. Do go on loving me as I love you, then we'll stop loving each other . . . [in French] Farewell, I hope that you would already have taken some French lessons, and I wouldn't doubt that – Listen: you would know better French than I because I certainly haven't written a word in this language in two years. Farewell. I kiss your hands, your face, your knees and your – at any rate, all that you permit me to kiss.

I am with all my heart
your
very affectionate Nephew and Cousin
Wolfg. Amadé Mozart

Honoré de Balzac to Ewelina Hánska,
19 June 1836

Here is the power of the letter. Balzac, author of the Comédie Humaine novels, begins his relationship with the Polish Countess Hánska without them ever having met. Daughter of a famous and rich aristocratic family, she married a landowner twenty-four years older than her and had five children by him. During the 1820s, she started to read Balzac's novels and in 1832, sent an anonymous letter from Poland to Paris. She is a fan and a married woman; he, a flattered and vain celebrity. After about a year they meet and begin their affair. Although Hánska's husband discovers their letters, Balzac is able to convince him that they are just a game.

When the count died in 1841, Balzac might have believed that the path was clear for the two of them to marry, but ill-health and financial worries meant that they did not wed until March 1850, just months before his own death in August. This letter from early in their relationship shows the near-obsession that Balzac has with Hánska, though there is a hint that her love is burning up his creative juices. If the husband had read this letter, would he have believed it was just a game?

MY BELOVED ANGEL,

I am nearly mad about you, as much as one can be mad: I cannot bring together two ideas that you do not interpose yourself between them. I can no longer think of nothing but you. In spite of myself, my imagination carries me to you. I grasp you, I kiss you, I caress you, a thousand of the most amorous caresses take possession of me. As for my heart,

there you will always be – very much so. I have a delicious
sense of you there. But my God, what is to become of me, if
you have deprived me of my reason? This is a monomania
which, this morning, terrifies me. I rise up every moment
say to myself, 'Come, I am going there!' Then I sit down
again, moved by the sense of my obligations. There is a
frightful conflict. This is not a life. I have never before been
like that. You have devoured everything. I feel foolish and
happy as soon as I let myself think of you. I whirl round in
a delicious dream in which in one instant I live a thousand
years. What a horrible situation! Overcome with love,
feeling love in every pore, living only for love, and seeing
oneself consumed by griefs, and caught in a thousand
spiders' threads. O, my darling Eva, you did not know it.
I picked up your card. It is there before me, and I talked
to you as if you were here. I see you, as I did yesterday,
beautiful, astonishingly beautiful. Yesterday, during the
whole evening, I said to myself 'She is mine!' Ah! The angels
are not as happy in Paradise as I was yesterday!

Picasso to Marie-Thérèse Walter, 19 July 1939

An obsessional commitment to art and love is the theme of this letter.
Pablo Picasso lived for his work and everything else in his life was sub-
ordinate to his frenzied mutating quest for artistic expression, often
inspired by his female muses. Olga Khokhlova, a Russian ballerina, was
his muse-lover during his synthetic cubism period; they married, but the
relationship did not last. He was forty-six and married to Olga when he
spotted seventeen-year-old blonde Marie-Thérèse Walter in the street.
They fell in love – though he remained married. Living between Paris
and a rented French country house, he painted her many times, and
she became the muse for some of his most joyous masterpieces such
as *Girl before a Mirror*, *Le Rêve* and *Nude in a Black Armchair*, a period of

intense creativity that reached a climax in the year 1932 at the Château de Boisgeloup in Normandy.

In bursts of colour, Marie-Thérèse appears blonde and sensuous. In 1935 she gives birth to their daughter Maya. This letter reflects in rhapsodic tones his almost carnivorous, all-consuming love for his young mistress. The 'problems in Switzerland' he refers to are probably business issues occasioned by the imminent outbreak of the Second World War.

But the artist was already focusing on his next muse, Dora Maar. Walter was highly jealous of the artist's new mistress: when the two girls met at his studio and demanded he choose one of them, he told them to fight it out – 'one of my choicest moments'. Marie-Thérèse lived on in Paris and survived the artist. Nine years after his death in 1973, she committed suicide.

My love,

I have just received your letter. I wrote several to you which you must have received by now. I love you more each day. You are everything to me. I will sacrifice everything for you, for our everlasting love. I Love you. I could never forget you my love and if I am unhappy it is because I don't belong to you as I would have liked. My Love, my Love, my Love, but I want for you to be happy and to think only of being happy. I would give anything for that. I am having some problems in Switzerland – but all that is not important. Let them send all the tears to me if I can prevent you from shedding one. I love you. Kiss Maya our daughter and I embrace you a thousand thousand times.

Yours,
Picasso.

John Keats to Fanny Brawne, 13 October 1819

Here is the ultimate celebration of all-consuming passion and doom-laden romanticism. John Keats, born in 1795, was cursed with ill-health, poverty and a desperation worthy of the outstanding Romantic poet. His mother died of tuberculosis when he was fourteen, and he felt surrounded by death on all sides.

In 1818 he meets Fanny Brawne who becomes the love of his life, but he is too poor to get engaged to her and their love is never consummated. His agonising obsessions with Fanny, love and death inspired the poems 'The Eve of St. Agnes' and 'La Belle Dame sans Merci' – also expressed in this letter to Fanny. Soon afterwards, Keats discovered that he too had tuberculosis and moved to Rome for his health, where he perished aged just twenty-six.

Fanny mourned him for six years, sharing her devotion with the poet's sister Fanny Keats. Finally Brawne got married to a Jewish merchant's son named Louis Lindon with whom she had a family. Just before her death in 1865, she revealed her relationship with Keats to her children and gave them his letters to her which would 'someday be considered of value'. The children published the letters, leading many to accuse Fanny of being unworthy of the poet. It was the much-later publication of her letters to Keats' sister that proved how she had cherished Keats' exquisite art.

25 College Street, Westminster

My dearest Girl,

This moment I have set myself to copy some verses out fair. I cannot proceed with any degree of content. I must write you a line or two and see if that will assist in dismissing you from my Mind for ever so short a time. Upon my Soul I can think of nothing else – The time is passed when I had power to advise and warn you against the unpromising morning of my Life – My love has made me selfish. I cannot exist without you – I am forgetful of every thing but seeing you again – my Life seems to stop there – I see no further. You have absorb'd me. I have a sensation at the present moment as though I was dissolving – I should be exquisitely miserable without the hope of soon seeing you. I should be afraid to separate myself far from you. My sweet Fanny, will your heart never change? My love, will it? I have no limit now to my love – Your note came in just here – I cannot be happier away from you – 'T is richer than an Argosy of Pearles. Do not threat me even in jest. I have been astonished that Men could die Martyrs for religion – I have shudder'd at it – I shudder no more. I could be martyr'd for my Religion – Love is my religion – I could die for that – I could die for you. My Creed is Love and you are its only tenet – You have ravish'd me away by a Power I cannot resist; and yet I could resist till I saw you; and even since I have seen you I have endeavoured often 'to reason against the reasons of my Love'. I can do that no more – the pain would be too great – My Love is selfish. I cannot breathe without you.

Yours for ever

John Keats

T.S. Eliot to George Orwell, 13 July 1944

Every writer dreads a rejection slip from a publisher. Here the publisher of Faber and Faber, who happens to be T.S. Eliot – better known as the poet of *The Waste Land* – pompously rejects the latest book by George Orwell, journalist, essayist and novelist. Orwell was best known at the time for having fought in the Spanish Civil War and for his brilliant work of reportage covering it published as *Homage to Catalonia*, as well as books on his personal experiences of poverty like *The Road to Wigan Pier*. But now he is doing something dangerous for any writer: changing his genre. In his latest work, he has used the metaphor of a farmyard to show how Soviet Russia – or a tyranny like it – becomes a murderous terror state. It is clearly an attack on Stalinism at a time when Stalin's Russia was an ally in the war against Hitler. Orwell was more sympathetic to Stalin's rival, Trotsky. Hence Eliot's point – missing the much wider message of the novel. *Animal Farm*, followed by his novel *1984*, were masterpieces that observed and warned against the Orwellian realities of modern politics that remain utterly relevant in the twenty-first century. Eliot's patronising rejection must rank as one of the most embarrassing mistakes in publishing history.

Dear Orwell

I know that you wanted a quick decision about 'Animal Farm': but the minimum is two directors' opinions, and that can't be done under a week. But for the importance of speed, I should have asked the Chairman to look at it as well. But the other director is in agreement with me on the main points. We agree that it is a distinguished piece of writing; that the fable is very skilfully handled, and that the narrative keeps one's interest on its own plane – and that is something very few authors have achieved since Gulliver.

On the other hand, we have no conviction (and I am sure none of the other directors would have) that this is the right point of view from which to criticise the political situation at the present time. It is certainly the duty of any publishing firm which pretends to other interests and motives than mere commercial prosperity, to publish books which go against the current of the moment: but in each instance that demands that at least one member of the firm should have the conviction that this is the thing that needs saying at the moment. I can't see any reason of prudence or caution to prevent anybody from publishing this book – if he believed in what it stands for.

Now I think my own dissatisfaction with this apologue is that the effect is simply one of negation. It ought to excite some sympathy with what the author wants, as well as sympathy with his objections to something: and the positive point of view, which I take to be generally Trotskyite, is not convincing. I think you split your vote, without getting any compensating stronger adhesion from either party – i.e. those who criticise Russian tendencies from the point of view of a purer communism, and those who, from a very different point of view, are alarmed about the future of small nations. And after all, your pigs are far more intelligent than the other animals, and therefore the best qualified to run the farm – in fact, there couldn't have been an Animal Farm at all without them: so that what was needed, (someone might argue), was not more communism but more public-spirited pigs.

I am very sorry, because whoever publishes this, will naturally have the opportunity of publishing your future work: and I have a regard for your work, because it is good writing of fundamental integrity.

Miss Sheldon will be sending you the script under separate cover.

Courage

Sarah Bernhardt to Mrs Patrick Campbell, 1915

She was the most famous actress of the late nineteenth and early twentieth century who could teach a lot to the celebrities of today. The beautiful daughter of a Parisian Jewish courtesan and an unknown client, Sarah Bernhardt was a self-made woman. One of her mother's lovers was Emperor Napoleon III's powerful half-brother the Duc de Morny, who helped her and may also have been the daughter's lover too.

Sarah was a free spirit as well as a brilliant thespian. When she had her only son, she refused to name the father, sometimes joking 'I could never make up my mind whether his father was [Premier] Gambetta, [novelist] Victor Hugo, or General Boulanger', though he was also possibly the son of her first love the Prince de Ligne. Either way, she became France's top actress, rich and grand, constantly touring – as this letter shows. When she fell fifteen feet from a balcony during a performance of *La Tosca* in Rio de Janeiro, she broke her knee. She tolerated the agony for years until, as she laconically confides here to another famous actress 'Mrs Pat', she decides aged seventy to do something about it once and for all . . .

Doctor will cut off my leg next Monday. Am very happy.
Kisses all my heart.
  Sarah Bernhardt.

Fanny Burney to her sister Esther, 22 March 1812

Frances 'Fanny' Burney, born in 1752, was the daughter of a highly cultured father – a composer and writer – and a French mother. In a long and eventful life, her literary gifts, her curiosity and sense of humour make her a ground-breaking woman in a man's world. Fanny started to write at a very young age, and she became one of the first bestselling female novelists at a time when well-born girls were not expected to dabble in disreputable storytelling. For this reason, she published her first novel *Evelina* anonymously, even trying conceal her female identity from the publisher. The witty satire on aristocratic society was a success and she became famous when her identity was revealed. While keeping a remarkable diary of personal and historical events from the age of sixteen to her death in 1840 and of course writing superb letters, Fanny went on to write a series of novels that helped inspire later writers like Jane Austen – her novel *Cecilia* was the source of the title of Austen's best-known novel: 'The whole of this unfortunate business,' says one of Fanny's characters, 'has been the result of pride and prejudice.'

Fanny had romances with various suitors but remained unmarried for a long time, turning down unappetising marriage proposals because she had 'no idea why the single life should not be happy. Liberty is not without its value – with woman as well as with men.' In 1785, Queen Charlotte, George III's wife, offered her the job of Keeper of the Robes and she became a courtier for five stressful years. She sympathised with the moderate ideas of the French Revolution, finally marrying an exiled general Alexandre d'Arblay who returned to his homeland to serve Napoleon. It is while living in Paris that Fanny notices a lump in her breast – and agrees to undergo a mastectomy, performed by Dr Dubois, the accoucheur of Napoleon's empress Marie-Louise, in the manner of a battlefield operation. Amazingly she survived, and lived on for almost thirty years. She describes every second of the agony in this unforgettable letter to her sister.

Account from
Paris of a Terrible
Operation – 1812

I have promised my dearest Esther a Volume – & here it is: I am at this moment quite well . . . Read, therefore, this narrative at your leisure, & without emotion – for all has ended happily . . .

About August, in the year 1810, I began to by annoyed by

a small pain in my breast, which went on augmenting from week to week, yet, being rather heavy than acute, without causing me any uneasiness with respect to consequences . . . Thus passed some months, during which Madame de Maisonneuve, my particularly intimate friend, joined with M. d'Arblay to press me to consent to an examination. I thought their fears groundless, and could not make so great a conquest over my repugnance. I relate this false confidence, now, as a warning to my dear Esther . . . M. d'A summoned a physician . . . he gave me some directions that produced no fruit – on the contrary, I grew worse, & M. d'A now would take no denial to my consulting M. Dubois, who had already attended & cured me in an abscess of which Maria, my dearest Esther, can give you the history. M. Dubois, the most celebrated surgeon of France, was then appointed accoucheur to the Empress . . . I began to perceive my real danger, M. Dubois gave me a prescription to be pursued for a month, during which time he could not undertake to see me again, & pronounced nothing – but uttered so many charges to me to be tranquil, & to suffer no uneasiness, that I could not but suspect there was room for terrible inquietude. . . . I took, but vainly, my prescription, & every symptom grew more serious . . .

A formal consultation now was held, of [doctors] Larrey, Ribe, & Moreau – and, in time, I was formally condemned to an operation by all Three. I was as much astonished as disappointed – for the poor breast was no where discoloured, & not much larger than its healthy neighbour. Yet I felt the evil to be deep, so deep, that I often thought if it could not be dissolved, it could only with life be extirpated. I called up, however, all the reason I possessed, or could assume, & told them that – if they saw no other alternative, I would not resist their opinion & experience: – the good Dr. Larrey, who, during his long attendance had conceived for me the warmest friendship, had now tears in his Eyes; from my dread he had expected resistance. . .

I strolled to the Sallon [on the day of surgery] – I saw it fitted with preparations, & I recoiled – But I soon returned; to what effect disguise from myself what I must so soon know? – yet the sight of the immense quantity of bandages, compresses, sponges, Lint – made me a little sick: – I walked backwards & forwards till I quieted all emotion, & became, by degrees, nearly stupid – torpid, without sentiment or consciousness; – & thus I remained till the Clock struck three . . . my room, without previous message, was entered by 7 Men in black, Dr Larry, M. Dubois, Dr Moreau, Dr Aumont, Dr Ribe, & a pupil of Dr Larry, & another of M. Dubois. I was now awakened from my stupor – & by a sort of indignation – Why so many? & without leave? – But I could not utter a syllable. M. Dubois acted as Commander in Chief. Dr Larry kept out of sight; M. Dubois ordered a Bed stead into the middle of the room. Astonished, I turned to Dr Larry, who had promised that an Arm Chair would suffice; but he hung his head, & would not look at me. Two old mattrasses M. Dubois then demanded, & an old Sheet. I now began to tremble violently, more with distaste & horror of the preparations even than of the pain. These arranged to his liking, he desired me to mount the Bed stead. I stood suspended, for a moment, whether I should not abruptly escape – I looked at the door, the windows – I felt desperate – but it was only for a moment, my reason then took the command, & my fears & feelings struggled vainly against it . . . I knew not, positively, then, the immediate danger, but every thing convinced me danger was hovering about me, & that this experiment could alone save me from its jaws. I mounted, therefore, unbidden, the Bed stead – & M. Dubois placed me upon the mattrass, & spread a cambric handkerchief upon my face. It was transparent, however, & I saw, through it, that the Bed stead was instantly surrounded by the 7 men & my nurse. I refused to be held; but when, Bright through the cambric, I saw the glitter of polished Steel – I closed my Eyes. I would not trust to convulsive fear the sight of the terrible incision. A silence the most profound ensued, which lasted for some minutes, during which, I imagine, they took their orders by signs, & made their examination – Oh what a horrible suspension! – I did not breathe . . . I feared they imagined the whole breast infected – feared it too justly, – for, again through the Cambric, I saw the hand of M. Dubois held up, while his forefinger first described a straight line from top to bottom of the breast, secondly a Cross, & thirdly a circle; intimating that the Whole was to be taken off . . . I closed once more my Eyes, relinquishing all watching, all resistance, all interference, & sadly resolute to be wholly resigned.

My dearest Esther, – & all my dears to whom she communicates this doleful ditty, will rejoice to hear that this resolution once taken, was firmly adhered to, in defiance of a terror that surpasses all description, & the most torturing pain. Yet – when the dreadful steel was plunged into the breast – cutting through veins – arteries – flesh – nerves – I needed no injunctions not to restrain my cries. I began a scream that lasted unintermittingly during the whole time of the incision – & I almost marvel that it rings not in my Ears still! so excruciating was the agony. When the wound was made, & the instrument was withdrawn, the pain seemed undiminished, for the air that suddenly rushed into those delicate parts felt like a mass of minute but sharp & forked poniards, that were tearing the edges of the wound – but when again I felt the instrument – describing a curve – cutting against the grain, if I may so say, while the flesh resisted in a manner so forcible as to oppose & tire the hand of the operator, who was forced to change from the right to the left – then, indeed, I thought I must have expired. I attempted no more to open my Eyes, – they felt as if hermetically shut, & so firmly closed, that the Eyelids seemed indented into the Cheeks. The instrument this second time withdrawn, I concluded the operation over – Oh no! presently the terrible cutting was renewed – & worse than ever, to separate the bottom, the foundation of this dreadful gland from the parts to which it adhered – Again all description would be baffled – yet again all was not over, – Dr Larry rested but his own hand, & – Oh Heaven! – I then felt the Knife rackling against the breast bone – scraping it! – This performed, while I yet remained in utterly speechless torture, I heard the Voice of Mr Larry, – (all others guarded a dead silence) in a tone nearly tragic, desire everyone present to pronounce if any thing more remained to be done; or if they thought the operation complete. The general voice was Yes, – but the finger of Mr Dubois – which I literally felt elevated over the wound, though I saw nothing, & though he touched nothing, so indescribably sensitive was the spot – pointed to some further requisition – & again began the scraping! – and, after this, Dr Moreau thought he discerned a peccant attom – and still, & still, M. Dubois demanded attom after attom. – My dearest Esther, not for days, not for Weeks, but for Months I could not speak of this terrible business without nearly again going through it! I could not think of it with impunity! I was sick, I was disordered by a single question – even now, 9 months after it is over, I have a head ache from going on with the account! & this miserable account, which I began 3 Months ago, at least, I dare not revise, nor read, the recollection is still so painful.

To conclude, the evil was so profound, the case so delicate, & the precautions necessary for preventing a return so numerous, that the operation, including the treatment and the dressing, lasted 20 minutes! a time, for sufferings so acute, that was hardly supportable – However, I bore it with all the courage I could exert, & never moved, nor stopt them, nor resisted, nor remonstrated, nor spoke – except once or twice . . . Twice, I believe, I fainted; at least, I have two total chasms in my memory of this transaction, that impede my tying together what passed. When all was done, & they lifted me up that I might be put to bed, my strength was so totally annihilated, that I was obliged to be carried, & could not even sustain my hands & arms, which hung as if I had been lifeless; while my face, as the Nurse has told me, was utterly colourless. This removal made me open my Eyes – & I then saw my good Dr Larry, pale nearly as myself, his face streaked with blood, & its expression depicting grief, apprehension, & almost horror.

David Hughes to his parents, 21 August 1940

Flight Lieutenant David Hughes was a pilot who served in the Battle of Britain, the air war that prevented a Nazi invasion and ensured British independence from Hitler's empire. The battle was won by the young pilots of the RAF, often aged just eighteen, many of whom were killed in the desperate fighting over England and the Channel. Posted near Newquay in Cornwall, Hughes' jaunty letter to his family tells of their excitements and fears.

It was Prime Minister Winston Churchill who best described the courage of those pilots in his famous speech: 'The gratitude of every home in our island, in our Empire, and indeed throughout the world, except in the abodes of the guilty, goes out to the British airmen who, undaunted by odds, unweakened by their constant challenge and mortal danger, are turning the tide of world war by their prowess and their devotion. Never in the field of human conflict was so much owed by so many to so few. All hearts go out to the fighter pilots.'

Less than a month after this letter, on 11 September 1940, Hughes was shot down over the English Channel; his body was never recovered.

RAF St Eval, Nr Newquay, Cornwall, 21 August 1940:

My Darlings,

It is a very long time since last I wrote, and very many things have happened.

I have shot and been shot at. I have killed, but not been killed. I have had my life saved by a comrade, and saved another in return.

I am now what is termed as an 'Ace', in that I have over 5 Jerries to my credit, namely 6 machines have been destroyed through my pressing a little button. For the boys' information I have shot down 3 ME 110's, 2 ME 109's, and a Dornier 17.

I arrived in my new Squadron on Sunday August 4th. There were three officers senior to me in the Squadron then. By August 11th I was the C.O. We lost twelve pilots in 4 days. After I took over we only lost one in a week, and had even greater odds against us. One day we were the first Squadron to make contact with the enemy, and I led my Squadron, twelve of us, against 350 Bombers escorted by 400 enemy fighters. It was one HELL of a scrap. When I landed I had 150 bullet holes in my machine, one was 1/2" from my head. I said a quick prayer before we dived to the attack, and I think my guardian angel was working overtime!!

On the 18th August our Squadron was sent down here for a rest, and we needed it. I'd lost a stone in under a fortnight. We had been flying for 6 and seven hours a day, missing meals, and averaging 5 hours sleep a day!

When we got here I had a telegram which read 'Congratulations 238 Squadron for the great part you have played' from Sir Cyril Newall, Air Chief Marshal.

Up to today we have had a quiet time here, but the Nazis gave us their attention today, and bombed us here. I was in the Mess when the bombs came, and rushed down to the machines and as I took off the Jerries machine gunned me, and then dodged into the clouds and got away.

I don't know when we shall return to Wallop, but I expect it will be soon.

I flew over to Cardiff last Monday and saw Joan [his wife] for a couple of hours. She has had a bad time recently, poor darling, her throat was bad again. I do love her so!!

I am writing this in flying kit and waiting for the word to take off.

Take care darlings.

All my love,

David.

Discovery

Ada Lovelace to Andrew Crosse, c.16 November 1844

Ada Lovelace was born in 1815, the daughter of the 'mad bad and dangerous to know' Romantic poet, Lord Byron. The poet had many illegitimate children but Ada was the only child of his marriage to Annabel Millbank. His scandalous conduct and political liberalism forced him to leave England just four months after she was born, never to meet her again: 'Is thy face like thy mother's, my fair child! ADA! sole daughter of my house and heart?' he wrote in Childe Harold's Pilgrimage. Byron died in Greece in 1824. Ada's mother denounced his many perversions and debaucheries for the rest of her life but showed little interest in Ada, who was brought up by her grandmother. She suffered headaches and near-paralysis after measles, and dreamed of designing a flying machine to fly away in – and escape her illness.

She was always fascinated by mathematics and science, showing a precocious talent in an age when few women were educated, let alone brilliant scientists in their own right. She had an affair and almost eloped with her tutor William Turner when she was seventeen, but three years later in 1835 she married Lord King, who became the Earl of Lovelace – giving her the fantastical title Countess of Lovelace – and they had three children. Ada's most important relationship was with her friend and mentor Charles Babbage (who called her 'Lady Fairy') and together they became pioneers of computing. Writing to her fellow scientist Andrew Crosse (with whose son John she probably had a love affair, beginning when he accompanied his father to the meeting referred to in this letter) from her home in Surrey, she calls herself 'the bride of science', explaining her modern philosophy of the interconnectivity of all nature and talking of her usual ill-health. Ada died at thirty-six from uterine cancer – the same age as her father, with whom she was buried.

Dear Mr Crosse, – Thank you for your kind and cordial letter . . . On Monday the 18th then, we expect you, and on Wednesday 20th we will all go to Broomfield. Perhaps you have felt already, from the tone of my letter, that I am more than ever now the bride of science. Religion to me is science, and science is religion. In that deeply-felt truth lies the secret of my intense devotion to the reading of God's natural works . . . And when I behold the scientific and so-called philosophers full of selfish feelings, and of a tendency to war against circumstances and Providence, I say to myself: They are not true priests, they are but half prophets – if not absolutely false ones. They have read the great page simply with the physical eye, and with none of the spirit within. The intellectual, the moral, the religious seem to be all naturally bound up and interlinked together in one great and harmonious whole . . . That God is one, and all that all the works and the feelings He has called into existence are ONE; this is a truth (a biblical and scriptural truth too) not in my opinion developed to the apprehension of most people in its really deep and unfathomable meaning. There is too much tendency to making separate and independent bundles of both the physical and the moral facts of the universe. Whereas, all and everything is naturally related and interconnected. A volume could I write on this subject . . . I think I may as well just give you a hint that I am subject at times to dreadful physical sufferings. If such should come over me at Broomfield, I may have to keep to my room for a time. In that case all I require is to be let alone. With all my wiry power and strength, I am prone at times to bodily sufferings, connected chiefly with the digestive organs, of no common degree or kind . . .

    Ever yours truly,
    AA Lovelace

Wilbur Wright to the Smithsonian Institution,
30 May 1899

A letter that flies. Enthusiasts of flight, not a pair of cranks, Wilbur Wright and his brother Orville were mechanics who produced their own brand of bicycle, but that was at many removes from an aeroplane. Yet they long dreamed of flight and practised the mechanics in their shop. It still seems extraordinarily unlikely, but when Wright, aged thirty-two, writes this letter, he is only three years from the first controlled flight . . .

The Smithsonian Institution,
Washington

Dear Sirs:

I have been interested in the problem of mechanical and human flight ever since as a boy I constructed a number of boats of various sizes after the style of Cayley's and Pénaud's machines. My observations since have only convinced me more firmly that human flight is possible and practicable. It is only a question of knowledge and skill just as in all acrobatic feats. Birds are the most perfectly trained gymnasts in the world and are specially well fitted for their work, and it may be that man will never equal them, but no one who has watched a bird chasing an insect or another bird can doubt that feats are performed which require three or four times the effort required in ordinary flight. I believe that simple flight at least is possible to man and that the experiments and investigations of a large number of independent workers will result in the accumulation of information and knowledge and skill which will finally lead to accomplished flight . . .

I am an enthusiast, but not a crank in the sense that I have some pet theories as to the proper construction of a flying machine. I wish to avail myself of all that is already known and then if possible add my mite to help on the future workers who will attain final success. I do not know the terms on which you send out your publications but if you will inform me of the cost I will remit the price.

Yours truly
Wilbur Wright

John Stevens Henslow to Charles Darwin, 24 August 1831

One of the foundation theories of modern biology starts with this letter. Charles Darwin said of his friend the Reverend John Stevens Henslow: 'I fully believe a better man never walked the earth.' The two met at Cambridge University in 1828, where Henslow was the Regius Professor of Botany, and became sufficiently good friends that Darwin was known as 'the man who walks with Henslow'. When Henslow hears of a place on an expedition led by Captain Robert FitzRoy aboard HMS Beagle to South America for two years, he thinks first of his protégé Darwin. The friend referred to in this letter, Marmaduke Ramsay, had proposed a trip to the Canary Islands, which Darwin would have attended had it not been for Ramsay's sudden death. This journey, which would last five years, gave Darwin the chance to research his ideas and led to his world-changing theory of evolution by natural selection, finally published in 1859 in *On the Origin of Species*.

My dear Darwin,

Before I enter upon the immediate business of this letter, let us condole together upon the loss of our inestimable friend poor Ramsay of whose death you have undoubtedly heard long before this. I will not now dwell upon this painful subject as I shall hope to see you shortly fully expecting that you will eagerly catch at the offer which is likely to be made you of a trip to Terra del Fuego & home by the

East Indies – I have been asked by Peacock who will read
& forward this to you from London to recommend him
a naturalist as companion to Capt FitzRoy employed by
Government to survey the S. extremity of America – I have
stated that I consider you to be the best qualified person I
know of who is likely to undertake such a situation – I state
this not on the supposition of yr. being a finished Naturalist,
but as amply qualified for collecting, observing, & noting
any thing worthy to be noted in Natural History. Peacock
has the appointment at his disposal & if he can not find a
man willing to take the office, the opportunity will probably
be lost – Capt. F. wants a man (I understand) more as a
companion than a mere collector & would not take any one
however good a Naturalist who was not recommended to
him likewise as a gentleman. Particulars of salary &c I know
nothing. The Voyage is to last 2 yrs. & if you take plenty of
Books with you, any thing you please may be done – You
will have ample opportunities at command – In short I
suppose there never was a finer chance for a man of zeal
& spirit. Capt F. is a young man. What I wish you to do is
instantly to come to Town & consult with Peacock (at No. 7
Suffolk Street Pall Mall East or else at the University Club) &
learn further particulars. Don't put on any modest doubts or
fears about your disqualifications for I assure you I think you
are the very man they are in search of – so conceive yourself
to be tapped on the Shoulder by your Bum-Bailiff & affecte
friend

    J. S. Henslow

Ferdinand and Isabella, King and Queen of Castile and Aragon, to Christopher Columbus, 30 March 1493

The letters that give Europeans their first glimpse of America. This marks the beginning of the age of empires in the Americas and their settlement by European colonists. The entire modern world starts with this letter accepting Spanish sovereignty. After much lobbying by the Genoan sailor and visionary Christopher Columbus, the 'Most Catholic Monarchs' of Spain, Ferdinand and Isabella, had finally permitted him to set sail expecting to find a route to India. On 3 August 1492 he embarked with ninety men. The Most Catholic Monarchs heard nothing until March 1493 when they received word that although he had lost one ship he had indeed discovered the Indies, seen the mainland of Asia (which in fact was today's Cuba), and founded a settlement on the island of Hispaniola (now Haiti and the Dominican Republic). On 30 March they reply with this letter, urging him to return to the court in Barcelona:

Sir Christopher Columbus, our admiral of the Ocean Sea and viceroy and governor of the islands that have been discovered in the Indies. We have seen your letters and were very pleased to learn about what you wrote to us in them and also that God has given you such a good ending to your efforts, guiding you well in what you began, by which He and we will be well served and our kingdoms will receive great benefit. May it please God that, besides serving Him in this, you will also receive because of it many favours from us that, rest assured, will be conferred on you as your services and labours merit.

We wish you to continue and carry forward what you have begun, with the help of God, and thus desire that you return immediately, because it is to our service that you hurry your return as much as possible in order to supply everything needed on time.

Christopher Columbus to Ferdinand and Isabella, 29 April 1493

Upon his return to Spain after his first voyage, Columbus writes a letter detailing 'the recently discovered Islands of India beyond the Ganges', addressed to the Royal Treasurer but meant for the monarchs Ferdinand and Isabella. It is later published. Famed for the 'discovery' of America, it was only new to Europeans: civilisations unknown to Europe had thrived there for millennia. Columbus was correct though that the Carib people were man-eating – and this letter describing them is the origin of the word 'cannibal'. Columbus believes he has reached the coast of China. Only Amerigo Vespucci later realised this was the New World.

As I know that it will afford you pleasure that I have brought my undertaking to a successful result, I have determined to write you this letter to inform you of everything that has been done and discovered in this voyage of mine.

On the thirty-third day after leaving Cadiz I came into the Indian Sea, where I discovered many islands inhabited by numerous people. I took possession of all of them for our most fortunate King by making public proclamation and unfurling his standard, no one making any resistance.

To the first of them I have given the name of our blessed Saviour, with whose aid I have reached this and all the rest; but the Indians call it Guanahani. To each of the others also I gave a new name, ordering one to be called Sancta Maria de Concepcion, another Fernandina, another Isabella, another Juana; and so with all the rest. As soon as we reached the island which I have just said was called Juana, I sailed along its coast some considerable distance towards the West, and found it to be so large, without any apparent end, that I believed it was not an island, but a continent, a province of

Cathay [China]. But I saw neither towns nor cities lying on the seaboard, only some villages and country farms, with whose inhabitants I could not get speech, because they fled as soon as they beheld us. I continued on, supposing I should come upon some city, or country-houses. At last, finding that no discoveries rewarded our further progress, and that this course was leading us towards the North, which I was desirous of avoiding, as it was now winter in these regions, and it had always been my intention to proceed Southwards, and the winds also were favourable to such desires, I concluded not to attempt any other adventures; so, turning back, I came again to a certain harbour, which I had remarked. From there I sent two of our men into the country to learn whether there was any king or cities in that land. They journeyed for three days, and found innumerable people and habitations, but small and having no fixed government; on which account they returned. Meanwhile I had learned from some Indians, whom I had seized at this place, that this country was really an island . . .

In the island, which I have said before was called Hispana, there are very lofty and beautiful mountains, great farms, groves and fields, most fertile both for cultivation and for pasturage, and well adapted for constructing buildings. The convenience of the harbours in this island, and the excellence of the rivers, in volume and salubrity, surpass human belief, unless one should see them . . . Besides, this Hispana abounds in various kinds of species, gold and metals. The inhabitants of both sexes of this and of all the other islands I have seen, or of which I have any knowledge, always go as naked as they came into the world, except that some of the women cover their private parts with leaves or branches, or a veil of cotton, which they prepare themselves for this purpose. They are all, as I said before, unprovided with any sort of iron, and they are destitute of arms, which

are entirely unknown to them, and for which they are
not adapted; not on account of any bodily deformity, for
they are well made, but because they are timid and full
of terror. They carry, however, canes dried in the sun in
place of weapons, upon whose roots they fix a wooded
shaft, dried and sharpened to a point. But they never dare
to make use of these; for it has often happened, when I
have sent two or three of my men to some of their villages
to speak with the inhabitants, that a crowd of Indians has
sallied forth; but when they saw our men approaching,
they speedily took to flight, parents abandoning children,
and children their parents. This happened not because any
loss or injury had been inflicted upon any of them. On the
contrary I gave whatever I had, cloth and many other things,
to whomsoever I approached, or with whom I could get
speech, without any return being made to me; but they are
by nature fearful and timid. But when they see that they
are safe, and all fear is banished, they are very guileless and
honest, and very liberal of all they have. No one refuses
the asker anything that he possesses; on the contrary they
themselves invite us to ask for it. They manifest the greatest
affection towards all of us, exchanging valuable things for
trifles, content with the very least thing or nothing at all. But
I forbade giving them a very trifling thing and of no value,
such as bits of plates, dishes, or glass; also nails and straps;
although it seemed to them, if they could get such, that they
had acquired the most beautiful jewels in the world . . . for
pieces of hoops, jugs, jars, and pots they bartered cotton and
gold like beasts. This I forbade, because it was plainly unjust;
and I gave them many beautiful and pleasing things, which
I had brought with me, for no return whatever, in order to
win their affection, and that they might become Christians
and inclined to love our King and Queen and Princes and all
the people of Spain; and that they might be eager to search

for and gather and give to us what they abound in and we
greatly need . . .

As soon as I had some into this sea, I took by force some
Indians from the first island, in order that they might learn
from us, and at the same time tell us what they knew about
affairs in these regions. This succeeded admirably; for in a
short time we understood them and they us both by gesture
and signs and words; and they were of great service to us.
They are coming now with me, and have always believed
that I have come from Heaven, notwithstanding the long
time they have been, and still remain, with us. They were
the first who told this wherever we went, one calling to
another, with a loud voice, Come, Come, you will see Men
from Heaven. Whereupon both women and men, children
and adults, young and old, laying aside the fear they had
felt a little before, flocked eagerly to see us, a great crowd
thronging about our steps, some bringing food, and others
drink, with greatest love and incredible good will . . .

I saw no monsters, neither did I hear accounts of any
such except in an island called Carib, the second as one
crosses over from Spain to India, which is inhabited by a
certain race regarded by their neighbours as very ferocious.
They eat human flesh, and make use of several kinds of
boats by which they cross over to all the Indian islands, and
plunder and carry off whatever they can. But they differ in
no respect from the others except in wearing their hair long
after the fashion of women. They make use of bows and
arrows made of reeds, having pointed shafts fastened to the
thicker portion, as we have before described. For this reason
they are considered to be ferocious, and the other Indians
consequently are terribly afraid of them; but I consider them
of no more account than the others. They have intercourse
with certain women who dwell alone upon the island of
Mateurin, the first as one crosses from Spain to India. These

women follow none of the usual occupations of their sex; but they use bows and arrows like those of their husbands, which I have described, and protect themselves with plates of copper, which is found in the greatest abundance among them . . .

Although these matters are very wonderful and unheard of, they would have been much more so, if ships to a reasonable amount had been furnished me. But what has been accomplished is great and wonderful, and not at all proportionate to my deserts, but to the sacred Christian faith, and to the piety and religion of our Sovereigns. For what is the mind of man could not compass the spirit of God has granted to mortals . . .

Therefore let King and Queen and Princes, and their most fortunate realms, and all other Christian provinces, let us all return thanks to our Lord and Saviour Jesus Christ, who has bestowed so great a victory and reward upon us . . . and let us be glad not only for the exaltation of our faith, but also for the increase of temporal prosperity, in which not only Spain but all Christendom is about to share.

As these things have been accomplished so have they been briefly narrated.

Farewell.

Tourism

Anton Chekhov to Anatoly Koni, 16 January 1891

In 1890 Anton Chekhov, a medical doctor as well as a celebrated writer, set off to the penal colony of Sakhalin in the Russian Far East, to conduct a census of its prisoners. His letters from there record the suffering and degeneracy of these godforsaken unfortunates and his own adventures, observing humanity with a world-weary and humorous sensitivity, and forensic precision.

To reach the 'Hell of Sakhalin', Chekhov travels by ship, river steamer, train and carriage. On the way he records the one-horse towns of the Far East. In one letter to his publisher Alexander Suvorin, he describes a visit to the brothel in Blagoveshchensk : 'a nice clean room sentimental in an Asiatic way furnished with bricabrac . . . The Japanese girl has her own concept of modesty. She doesn't put out the light and when you ask what the Japanese is for one thing or another she gives a straight answer as she does so because she doesn't understand much Russian, points her fingers, and even puts her hand on it. What's more she doesn't put on airs or go all coy like Russian women. And all the time she is laughing . . . She is amazingly skilled at her job so that you feel you are not having intercourse but taking part in a top level equitation class. When you come ,the Japanese girl pulls with her teeth a sheet of cotton wool from her sleeve, catches you by the 'boy', gives you a massage . . . All this is done with coquetry, laughing, singing and saying tsu.'

Born in Taganrog on the Sea of Azov, Chekhov had endured a hard childhood, but after qualifying as a doctor he started to write stories for Suvorin's newspaper. He became even more famous for plays like The Cherry Orchard and Uncle Vanya, describing the key to the art of drama: 'Remove everything that has no relevance to the story. If you say in the first chapter that there is a rifle hanging on the wall, in the second or third chapter it absolutely must go off. If it's not going to be fired, it shouldn't be hanging there.' After a raffish love life, forswearing marriage, he married late – but was only forty-four when he died of tuberculosis. He liked to claim 'medicine is my wife, literature is my

mistress, but this letter to his friend and lawyer Koni combines the two
– it is one of his best.

DEAR SIR, ANATOLY FYODOROVITCH [KONI]
I did not hasten to answer your letter because I am not
leaving Petersburg before next Saturday. I am sorry I have
not been to see Madame Naryshkin, but I think I had better
defer my visit till my book has come out, when I shall be
able to turn more freely to the material I have. My brief
Sahalin past looms so immense in my imagination that when
I want to speak about it I don't know where to begin, and it
always seems to me that I have not said what was wanted.

I will try and describe minutely the position of the
children and young people in Sakhalin. It is exceptional.
I saw starving children, I saw girls of thirteen prostitutes,
girls of fifteen with child. Girls begin to live by prostitution
from twelve years old, sometimes before menstruation
has begun. Church and school exist only on paper, the
children are educated by their environment and the convict
surroundings. Among other things I have noted down a
conversation with a boy of ten years old. I was making
the census of the settlement of Upper Armudano; all the
inhabitants are poverty-stricken, every one of them, and
have the reputation of being desperate gamblers at the game
of shtoss. I go into a hut; the people are not at home; on a
bench sits a white-haired, round-shouldered, bare-footed
boy; he seems lost in thought. We begin to talk.

I. 'What is your father's second name?'
He. 'I don't know.'
I. 'How is that? You live with your father and don't know
what his name is? Shame!'
He. 'He is not my real father.'
I. 'How is that?'

He. 'He is living with mother.'

I. 'Is your mother married or a widow?'

He. 'A widow. She followed her husband here.'

I. 'What has become of her husband, then?'

He. 'She killed him.'

I. 'Do you remember your father?'

He. 'No, I don't, I am illegitimate. I was born when mother was at Kara.'

On the Amur steamer going to Sakhalin, there was a convict with fetters on his legs who had murdered his wife. His daughter, a little girl of six, was with him. I noticed wherever the convict moved the little girl scrambled after him, holding on to his fetters. At night the child slept with the convicts and soldiers all in a heap together. I remember I was at a funeral in Sakhalin. Beside the newly dug grave stood four convict bearers ex officio; the treasury clerk and I, in the capacity of Hamlet and Horatio, wandering about the cemetery; the dead woman's lodger, a Circassian, who had come because he had nothing better to do; and a convict woman who had come out of pity and had brought the dead woman's two children, one a baby, and the other, Alyoshka, a boy of four, wearing a woman's jacket and blue breeches with bright-coloured patches on the knees. It was cold and damp, there was water in the grave, the convicts were laughing. The sea was in sight. Alyoshka looked into the grave with curiosity; he tried to wipe his chilly nose, but the long sleeve of his jacket got into his way. When they began to fill in the grave I asked him: 'Alyoshka, where is your mother?' He waved his hand with the air of a gentleman who has lost at cards, laughed, and said: 'They have buried her!'

The convicts laughed, the Circassian turned and asked what he was to do with the children, saying it was not his duty to feed them.

Infectious diseases I did not meet with in Sakhalin. There is very little congenital syphilis, but I saw blind children, filthy, covered with eruptions – all diseases that are evidence of neglect. Of course I am not going to settle the problem of the children. I don't know what ought to be done.

Gustave Flaubert to Louis Bouilhet, 15 January 1850

This letter of sexual adventure is by Gustave Flaubert, the French novelist, to his schoolfriend and fellow writer Louis Bouilhet. In 1849–50, aged around thirty, Flaubert travels through the Middle East, from Greece to Istanbul and Beirut, sightseeing and experiencing as much as he could in the backstreets and bathhouses. His letters describe encounters with girls and boys, joking that he travels for 'educational purposes'. His risky adventures cost him dear – he was tormented for the rest of his life by the infections he contracted there and this contributed to his decision not to marry or have children.

On his return, he started work on his masterpiece, *Madame Bovary*, the story of a disastrous adulterous affair. He prided himself on his search for the precise word in his writing – 'la mot juste' – exhausting himself with this exacting perfectionism that meant he published many fewer works than his equals, Balzac and Zola. But even in this letter, set in a Cairo bathhouse, the wit is as acute as the style is meticulous.

. . . Speaking of bardashes, this is what I know about them. Here it is quite accepted. One admits one's sodomy, and it is spoken of at table in the hotel. Sometimes you do a bit of denying, and then everybody teases you and you end up confessing. Travelling as we are for educational purposes, and charged with a mission by the government, we have considered it our duty to indulge in this form of ejaculation. So far the occasion has not presented itself. We continue to seek it, however. It's at the baths that such things take place. You reserve the bath for yourself (five francs including masseurs, pipe, coffee, sheet and towel) and you skewer your lad in one of the rooms. Be informed, furthermore, that all the bath-boys are bardashes. The final masseurs, the ones who come to rub you when all the rest is done, are usually quite nice young boys. We had our eye on one in an establishment very near our hotel. I reserved the bath exclusively for myself. I went, and the rascal was away that day! I was alone in the hot room, watching the daylight fade through the great circles of glass in the dome. Hot water was flowing everywhere; stretched out indolently I thought of a quantity of things as my pores tranquilly dilated. It is very voluptuous and sweetly melancholy to take a bath like that quite alone, lost in those dim rooms where the slightest noise reverberates like cannon shot, while the naked kellaks call out to one another as they massage you, turning you over like embalmers preparing you for the tomb. That day (the day before yesterday, Monday), my kellak was rubbing me gently, and when he came to the noble parts he lifted up my boules d'amour to clean them, then continuing to rub my chest with his left hand, he began to pull with his right on my prick, and as he drew it up and down, he leaned over my shoulder and said 'baksheesh, baksheesh'. He was a man in his fifties, ignoble, disgusting – imagine the effect, and the word 'baksheesh, baksheesh'. I pushed him away a little, saying 'làh, làh' (no, no) – he thought I was angry and took on a craven look – then I gave him a few pats on the shoulder, saying 'làh, làh' again but more gently – he smiled a smile that meant 'You're not fooling me – you like it as much as anybody, but today you've decided against it for some reason.' As for me, I laughed aloud like a dirty old man and the shadowy vault of the bath echoed with the sound . . .

War

Peter the Great to Catherine I, 27 June 1709

This letter marks the moment that Russia becomes a world power – the triumph every Russian leader from Stalin to Putin aspires to emulate. Peter the Great was the six-foot-seven-inch tsar who, in 1707, faced an invasion from the best army of the day, Sweden. But he fought back, founded a new capital – St Petersburg – and created a new navy and army. Finally, on this day in 1709 at Poltava, he defeats the Swedes and wants to share the moment with his wife.

She too is an extraordinary individual. She had been a laundress, mistress of many generals, and was not even a Russian; but Peter fell in love with her, changed her name to Catherine, and ultimately would make her empress of Russia in her own right. In their saucy letters he calls her 'Katerinushka, my heart's friend' often adding 'I am bored without you.' They would tease each other about other girls – especially laundresses. 'I got your letter full of jokes. You'll say I'll be looking for a new lady but I am too old,' he writes to her when visiting Versailles on 28 April 1717.

'I think Your Worship is distracted by a multitude of fountains and forgets us,' she jokes back on 25 May, with much phallic imagery. 'Though I think you have found new laundresses, your old laundress hasn't forgotten you.'

Joshing about sex and his frequent affliction, venereal disease, he remarks, 'The doctors ban domestic fun. I've sent my mistress away for I won't be able to resist the temptation if I kept her here.' To which Catherine replies, 'I hope the mistress's admirer [Peter] will arrive in the same state of health as she did!' adding, 'But if my old man was here we'd make us another kid.' They had around twelve children together but all the boys died. On 2 January 1717 he celebrates a new son: 'I received your delightful letter in which you say the Lord God has blessed us by giving us another recruit.' The very next day, hearing the baby has died, he tries to console his wife : 'I received your letter about what I knew before, the unexpected occurrence which has changed joy to grief. What answer can I give except that of the long-suffering Job? The Lord has given and the Lord has taken away; Blessed be the name of the Lord. I beg you to reflect on it in this way; I do as far as I can.'

So this partner is the person with whom he wishes to share his world-changing victory at Poltava, writing to her:

Matushka, good day. I declare to you that the all-merciful God has this day granted us an unprecedented victory over the enemy. In a word, the whole of the enemy's army is knocked on the head, about which you will hear from us.

Peter

PS Come here and congratulate us!

Napoleon to Josephine, 3 December 1805

This is the letter of a man who has just defeated the emperors of Russia and Austria and is now the master of Europe. On the battlefield of Austerlitz, Napoleon scribbles the following note to his wife Josephine.

To the Empress, at Strasbourg,

I have sent Lebrun to you from the battlefield. I defeated the Russian and Austrian army commanded by the two emperors. I am slightly [!] tired, as I spent eight days in a bivouac out in the open and the nights were rather cold. Tonight, I am staying at the palace of Prince Kaunitz, where I shall sleep two or three hours. The Russian army is not only defeated, it is destroyed.

I kiss you,

Napoleon.

Dwight D. Eisenhower to all Allied troops, 5 June 1944

On 5 June 1944, General 'Ike' Eisenhower, Supreme Allied Commander of the Allied Expeditionary Force and later President of the United States, gives the order to launch the long-awaited Operation Overlord, the invasion of Nazi-occupied France. It is risky: an assault across the Channel with overwhelming force but against the well-defended coast of Hitler's Atlantic Wall – and at the mercy of weather and sea and Nazi airpower. On that day Eisenhower writes one letter to be issued to all the troops before the assault. But he also writes a second one, to be issued in the event of a disaster, wrongly dated 5 July. Fortunately, this letter was never sent. D-Day was successful. Here is the first:

You are about to embark upon a great crusade, toward which we have striven these many months. The eyes of the world are upon you . . . We will accept nothing less than full victory! Good Luck!

And this is the letter never sent:

5 July

Our landings in the Cherbourg–Havre area have failed to gain a satisfactory foothold and I have withdrawn the troops. My decision to attack at this time and place was based upon the best information available. The troops, the air and the Navy did all that Bravery and devotion to duty could do. If any blame or fault attaches to the attempt it is mine alone.

Catherine, Duchess of Oldenburg to her brother Alexander I, 3 September 1812

In the summer of 1812, the French emperor Napoleon invaded Russia. By September he had taken the ancient capital of Moscow, which was then burned to the ground, a shocking humiliation for Tsar Alexander I and the Russian people. At this moment of disaster, Alexander trusts no one and knows his reputation, if not his actual life, is in peril. He is encouraged in his determination to resist at all costs – even if he has to retreat all the way back to the city of Kazan – by the person he loves most of all: his strong and fearless sister Catiche. This letter is as powerful as it is short.

Moscow is taken. Some things are beyond comprehension. Don't forget your resolve, 'no peace', and you have still the hope of regaining your honour. If you are in sorrow don't forget your friends ready to fly to you and too happy if they can be any help: command them.

My dear friend, no peace, and if you get to Kazan, still no peace!

Philip II to the Duke of Medina Sidonia, 1 July 1588

A letter encouraging a reluctant servant to perform a thankless task of extraordinary magnitude.

Philip of Spain was the most powerful king in Europe at the time, ruler of an empire on which the sun never set – but Queen Elizabeth of England defied him. First he had asked her to marry him, then he ordered her assassination, and finally he contrived his Great Enterprise: the invasion of England by his 'Great and Most Fortunate Navy' – the Spanish Armada – carrying 27,000 men in a hundred and thirty warships that were to collect en route, as the invasion force, a further 30,000 waiting in the Spanish Netherlands. Philip gave the command to an experienced admiral, the Marqués de Santa Cruz, but he died before the fleet set off, and the king ordered the Duke of Medina Sidonia to take his place. The duke, no sailor, knew the plan was faulty, so he tried to back out: 'Your Majesty, believe me when I assure you that we are very weak . . . how do you think we can attack so great a country as England with such a force as ours is now?'

This is Philip's reply. The Armada sailed on 28 May 1588 and was a disaster.

Duke and cousin.

I have received the letter written in your hand, dated 24 June. From what I know of you, I believe you have brought all these matters to my attention solely because of your zeal to serve me and the desire to succeed in your command. The certainty that this is so prompts me to be franker with you than I should be with another . . . If this were an unjust war, one could indeed take the tempest as a sign from Our Lord to cease offending Him; but being as just as it is, one cannot believe that He will disband it, but will rather grant it more favour than we could hope . . . I have dedicated this enterprise to God . . . Pull yourself together, then, and do your part.

Philip.

Harun al-Rashid to Nikephoros I, AD 802

Harun al-Rashid was the fifth and most famous Abbasid Caliph – formally the Emir al-Muamimin, or Commander of the Faithful, ruling the vast Islamic empire from Baghdad. He is the caliph who appears in *The Thousand and One Nights*. When he is defied by the Byzantine emperor Nikephoros who refuses to pay tribute, the Caliph sends this laconic reply – promising war.

In the name of God, the Merciful, the Compassionate, from Harun the Commander of the Faithful to Nikephoros the dog of the Byzantines: O son of an infidel woman, I have read your letter, and the reply is what you will see, without you having to hear it. Farewell!

Rasputin to Nicholas II, 17 July 1914

Perhaps the most outspoken letter ever written to a tsar by a peasant. In July 1914, Europe slides towards to war. Tsar Nicholas is reluctant to fight, yet fears that Russia cannot avoid conflict and remain a great power. His wife Alexandra is with him but he excludes her from discussions, fearing her hysteria. Their sacred adviser the peasant Rasputin is far from the capital, recovering from an attempt to kill him, but when Alexandra discovers Russia is close to war, she telegraphs him, begging him to appeal to the tsar. This is the letter Rasputin sends by telegram, warning of catastrophe if Russia should fight. Nicholas was outraged by Rasputin's impertinence – yet he was right. And Nicholas kept the letter until his own murder in 1918.

Dear friend

I'll say again a menacing cloud is over Russia, lots of sorrow and grief, it's dark and there's not a ray of hope. A sea of tears, immeasurable, and as to blood? What can I say? There are no words, indescribable horror. I know they all want war from you, evidently not realising that this means ruin. Hard is God's punishment when he takes away reason, it's the beginning of the end. You are the Tsar Father of the people, don't allow the madmen to triumph and destroy themselves and the people. Yes, they'll conquer Germany, but what of Russia? If one thinks then truly never for all of time has one suffered like Russia, drowned in her own blood. Great will be the ruin, grief without end.

Grigory

Blood

Paiankh to Nodjmet, c.1070 BC

Murder by letter. The military dictator of Thebes, Paiankh ruled with his wife Nodjmet. In an early case of state killing, while Paiankh is away fighting rebellious Nubia, he has left his wife Nodjmet in charge. When she scents treason at home she asks his advice. Paiankh's reply is unequivocal and chilling: disappear them!

Have these two watchmen brought to my house and get to the bottom of their words in short order, then have them killed and thrown into the water by night.

Vladimir Lenin to the Bolsheviks of Penza, 11 August 1918

Here is the real Lenin as the Soviet people never saw him.

Vladimir Lenin became Soviet premier when he led the Bolshevik seizure of power in October 1917. During his rule and after his death he was promoted in propaganda as a benign grandfatherly patriarch, his body preserved and revered in a mausoleum like a saint. On the contrary, Lenin prided himself on his harshness and often said, 'A revolution without firing squads is meaningless.' When he heard that Stalin had killed people he said, 'That's exactly the type we need.' As soon as Lenin took power he created the ruthless Cheka, the secret police, to enforce his terror; and as his regime struggles to win the civil war he sends letters like this, ordering random killings. This letter was only revealed after the fall of the Soviet Union in 1991. His body still remains on show in Red Square.

Comrades! The insurrection of five kulak districts should be pitilessly suppressed. The interests of the whole revolution require this because 'the last decisive battle' with the kulaks is now underway <u>everywhere</u>. An example must be demonstrated.

1. Hang (and make sure that the hanging takes place <u>in full view of the people</u>) <u>no fewer than one hundred</u> known kulaks, rich men, bloodsuckers.
2. Publish their names.
3. Seize <u>all</u> their grain from them.
4. Designate hostages in accordance with yesterday's telegram.

Do it in such a fashion that for hundreds of kilometres around the people might see, tremble, know, shout: <u>they are strangling</u> and will strangle to death the bloodsucking kulaks.

Telegraph receipt and <u>implementation</u>.

Yours, Lenin.

Find some truly hard people.

Josef Stalin to Kliment Voroshilov, 3 July 1937

In February 1937, Stalin unleashed the Great Terror, directed mainly at his own comrades in the Communist Party. Around a million innocent people were eventually shot, millions more imprisoned. In public he remains elusive as the arrests and executions intensify, but privately he is directing every detail, and many of his letters to his henchmen, encouraging the slaughter, survive: 'Isn't it time to squeeze this gentleman and force him to report on this dirty business?' he writes during the torture of one prisoner. At other times he sends peremptory letters like this one to a trusted acolyte: 'Comrade Malenkov. Moskvin must be arrested. J.St.' When his killers become exhausted, he urges them on: 'The sharper the teeth the better. J.St.'

He convinces his comrades that the arrested are guilty by showing them confessions, secured by torture. Here he sends these testimonies to a henchman with this covering letter:

Dear Klim, did you read the testimonies . . .? How do you like the bourgeois puppies of Trotsky . . .? They wanted to wipe out all the members of the Politburo . . . isn't it weird? How low can people sink? J.St.

Mao Zedong to the Red Guards of Tsinghua University Middle School, 1 August 1966

Here is the letter unleashing the chaos and cruelty of the Cultural Revolution. Since seizing power in 1949, Mao had killed millions of 'class enemies' by shooting and by famine but now, directing a campaign behind the scenes backed by henchmen like his wife Jiang Qing and his defence minister, Lin Biao, Mao turns the guns on his own over-mighty officials who had tried to restrain his power. His weapons are the young student radicals and thugs of the Red Guards, whom he uses to destroy any rivals by inciting mob violence or, as he calls it, 'bombarding the headquarters'.

This letter is one of the public signs of his support for the Red Guards: 'it is right to rebel against reactionaries.' He suggests that 'after their mistakes have been pointed out', their victims should be offered the chance to become 'new men'. This is sinister doubletalk: many were tortured, killed or 're-educated' in the countryside.

Red Guard Comrades
I have received both the big-character posters which you sent on 28 July as well as the letter which you sent me, asking for an answer. The big-character posters express your anger at and denunciation of all landlords, bourgeois,

imperialists, revisionists and their running dogs who exploit and oppress the workers, peasants, revolutionary intellectuals and revolutionary parties and groupings. You say it is right to rebel against reactionaries: I enthusiastically support you . . . Here I want to say that I myself as well as my revolutionary comrades-in-arms all take the same attitude. No matter where they are, in Peking or anywhere in China, I will give enthusiastic support to all who take an attitude similar to yours in the Cultural Revolution movement. Another thing, while supporting you, at the same time we ask you to pay attention to uniting with all who can be united with. As for those who have committed serious mistakes, after their mistakes have been pointed out you should offer them a way out of their difficulties by giving them work to do, and enabling them to correct their mistakes and become new men. Marx said: the proletariat must emancipate not only itself but all mankind. If it cannot emancipate all mankind, then the proletariat itself will not be able to achieve final emancipation. Will comrades please pay attention to this truth too.

China descended into four years of state-sanctioned anarchy, with Chairman Mao emerging omnipotent. He promoted Lin Biao as his chosen heir but then he started to turn on his second-in-command. Marshal Lin planned Mao's assassination before attempting to flee to Russia, and was killed on 13 September 1971 when his plane crashed. In the ensuing search for enemies, Mao wrote this short note advising deputy chief bodyguard Zhang Yao-ci how to survive. The reference to 'operas and films' shows Mao withdrawing support from his radical wife Jiang Qing, who controlled the arts – and ending the Cultural Revolution. The letter reveals the bleak state of paranoia and terror at the court of one of the twentieth century's monsters – in his own words.

1. Don't cultivate connections;

2. Don't visit people;
3. Don't give dinners or gifts;
4. Don't invite people to operas or films;
5. Don't have photographs taken with people.

Josip Broz Tito to Josef Stalin, 1948

The letter that terrified the most terrifying leader of modern times. When a schism grows between the Communist allies the Soviet Union and Yugoslavia, Soviet leader Stalin expects the smaller country to bow before his power. Instead, the Yugoslav President Marshal Tito defies Stalin, who is incensed. He sends assassins to murder Tito but they repeatedly fail. Finally the Yugoslavian sends this note to Stalin, who supposedly kept it with a few other special letters in his personal safe where it was found after his death. It worked. Stalin stopped sending assassins.

Stop sending people to kill me! We've already captured five of them one of them with a bomb and another with a rifle . . . If you don't stop sending killers, I'll send a very fast-working one to Moscow and I certainly won't have to send another.

Destruction

Theobald von Bethman-Hollwegg to Count Leopold Berchtold, 6 July 1914

This is the letter that launches the slaughter of the First World War. Reading its mannered language from the age of emperors and courts, it is hard to grasp the killing machine that it unleashed. Germany deserves blame but Austria, Serbia and Russia also share that responsibility. On 28 June 1914, Serbian terrorists, secretly backed by the Serbian government, kill Archduke Franz Ferdinand, heir to the Austro-Hungarian throne. In retaliation, Austria wishes to destroy Serbia, but the latter is backed by Russia, and Russia is backed France – and they are both backed by Britain. Many Austrian and German potentates believe that war would deliver the best chance to defeat Russia but Austria cannot risk it without the support of its more powerful German ally. Austrian Foreign Secretary Berchtold agrees with his master Emperor Franz Josef that Serbian destruction is essential.

On 5 July, Berchtold sends his chief of staff Count Alexander von Hoyos to Berlin to get German backing. At lunch with the German kaiser Wilhelm II, the Austrian ambassador delivers Franz Josef's letter that argues 'the attack on my poor nephew' was 'no longer an affair at Sarajevo of the single bloody deed of an individual but a well-organised conspiracy of which the threads lead to Belgrade.' The kaiser promises Germany's 'faithful support' even if Russia intervenes, a policy confirmed by his Chancellor Bethman-Hollweg in this letter: the early paragraphs concern Austria's wish to move away from Romania (ruled by a king closely related to the German kaiser) but the last two lines are decisive – the so-called Blank Cheque. The Germans grossly underestimate the Russian determination to defend Serbia, the French and British determination to back the Russians and finally the British determination to back their French and Russian allies. By the time the Germans realise the scale of their miscalculation, it is too late. The war, which began on 28 July, would kill around 16 million people.

Confidential – For Your Excellency's personal information
and guidance
Berlin
6 July 1914

The Austro-Hungarian Ambassador yesterday delivered to
the Emperor a confidential personal letter from the Emperor
Francis Joseph, which depicts the present situation from the
Austro-Hungarian point of view, and describes the measures
which Vienna has in view . . .

I replied to Count Szagyeny today on behalf of His
Majesty that His Majesty sends his thanks to the Emperor
Francis Joseph for his letter and would soon answer it
personally.

In the meantime His Majesty desires to say that he is
not blind to the danger which threatens Austria-Hungary
and thus the Triple Alliance as a result of the Russian and
Serbian Pan-Slavic agitation.

Even though His Majesty is known to feel no unqualified
confidence in Bulgaria and her ruler, and naturally inclines
more toward our old ally Romania and her Hohenzollern
prince, yet he quite understands that the Emperor Francis
Joseph, in view of the attitude of Romania and of the danger
of a new Balkan alliance aimed directly at the Danube
Monarchy, is anxious to bring about an understanding
between Bulgaria and the Triple Alliance.

[. . .]

His Majesty will, furthermore, make an effort at
Bucharest, according to the wishes of the Emperor Francis
Joseph, to influence King Carol to the fulfilment of the
duties of his alliance, to the renunciation of Serbia, and to
the suppression of the Romanian agitations directed against
Austria-Hungary.

Finally, as far as concerns Serbia, His Majesty, of course, cannot interfere in the dispute now going on between Austria-Hungary and that country, as it is a matter not within his competence.

The Emperor Francis Joseph may, however, rest assured that His Majesty will faithfully stand by Austria-Hungary, as is required by the obligations of his alliance and of his ancient friendship.

Bethmann-Hollweg

Harry Truman to Irv Kupcinet, 5 August 1963

President Harry Truman ordered the use of America's new nuclear bombs to accelerate the end of the war against Japan. On 6 and 9 August 1945, the atomic bombs dropped on Hiroshima and then Nagasaki – causing a vast loss of life – successfully forced Japan to sue for peace. They also heralded the start of a new and terrifying era of nuclear proliferation, intensifying in the twenty-first century as less stable states such as Pakistan and North Korea become nuclear powers. Never has the fear of nuclear apocalypse been so real. That makes this letter by the retired President feel very relevant. The then seventy-nine-year-old Truman, living in retirement in Missouri, writes to the columnist Irv 'Kup' Kupcinet, who has published an article supporting his actions in the *Chicago Sun-Times*. The letter reveals the matter-of-fact, no-nonsense style of the unpretentious ex-haberdasher who, as President, kept a sign on his desk that read: THE BUCK STOPS HERE.

Dear Kup:

I appreciated most highly your column of July 30th, a copy of which you sent me.

I have been rather careful not to comment on the articles that have been written on the dropping of the bomb for the simple reason that the dropping of the bomb was completely and thoroughly explained in my Memoirs, and it was done to save 125,000 youngsters on the American side and 125,000 on the Japanese side from getting killed and that is what it did. It probably also saved a half million youngsters on both sides from being maimed for life.

You must always remember that people forget, as you said in your column, that the bombing of Pearl Harbor was done while we were at peace with Japan and trying our best to negotiate a treaty with them. All you have to do is to go out and stand on the keel of the Battleship in Pearl Harbor with the 3,000 youngsters underneath it who had no chance whatever of saving their lives. That is true of two or three other battleships that were sunk in Pearl Harbor. Altogether, there were between 3,000 and 6,000 youngsters killed at that time without any declaration of war. It was plain murder.

I knew what I was doing when I stopped the war that would have killed a half million youngsters on both sides if those bombs had not been dropped. I have no regrets and, under the same circumstances, I would do it again – and this letter is not confidential.

Sincerely yours,
Harry Truman

Disaster

Pliny the Younger to Tacitus, c.AD 106/107

On 24 August AD 79 Mount Vesuvius erupted, destroying the nearby towns of Pompeii and Herculaneum entirely. The lawyer and writer Pliny the Younger was eighteen years old at the time of the eruption, which resulted in the death of his uncle Pliny the Elder. Young Pliny and his mother managed to escape. Around a quarter of a century later, Pliny's friend, the historian Tacitus, asks him to supply details of the event. Pliny's letter is a masterpiece of reportage.

You ask me to send you an account of my uncle's death, so that you may be able to give posterity an accurate description of it. I am much obliged to you, for I can see that the immortality of his fame is well assured, if you take in hand to write of it. For although he perished in a disaster which devastated some of the fairest regions of the land, and though he is sure of eternal remembrance like the peoples and cities that fell with him in that memorable calamity, though too he had written a large number of works of lasting value, yet the undying fame of which your writings are assured will secure for him a still further lease of life. For my own part, I think that those people are highly favoured by Providence who are capable either of performing deeds worthy of the historian's pen or of writing histories worthy of being read, but that they are peculiarly favoured who can do both. Among the latter I may class my uncle, thanks to his own writings and to yours. So I am all the more ready to fulfil your injunctions, nay, I am even prepared to beg to be allowed to undertake them.

My uncle was stationed at Misenum, where he was in active command of the fleet, with full powers. On the 24th of August, about the seventh hour, my mother drew his attention to the fact that a cloud of unusual size and shape had made its appearance. He had been out in the sun, followed by a cold bath, and after a light meal he was lying down and reading. Yet he called for his sandals, and climbed up to a spot from which he could command a good view of the curious phenomenon. Those who were looking at the cloud from some distance could not make out from which mountain it was rising – it was afterwards discovered to have been Mount Vesuvius – but in likeness and form it more closely resembled a pine-tree than anything else, for what corresponded to the trunk was of great length and height, and then spread out into a number of branches, the reason being, I imagine, that while the vapour was fresh, the cloud was borne upwards, but when the vapour became wasted, it lost its motion, or even became dissipated by its own weight, and spread out laterally. At times it looked white, and at other times dirty and spotted, according to the quantity of earth and cinders that were shot up.

To a man of my uncle's learning, the phenomenon appeared one of great importance, which deserved a closer study. He ordered a Liburnian galley to be got ready, and offered to take me with him, if I desired to accompany him, but I replied that I preferred to go on with my studies, and it so happened that he had assigned me some writing to do. He was just leaving the house when he received a written message from Rectina, the wife of Tascus, who was terrified at the peril threatening her – for her villa lay just beneath the mountain, and there were no means of escape save by shipboard – begging him to save her from her perilous position. So he changed his plans, and carried out with the greatest fortitude the task, which he had started as a scholarly inquiry.

He had the galleys launched and went on board himself, in the hope of succouring, not only Rectina, but many others, for there were a number of people living along the shore owing to its delightful situation. He hastened, therefore, towards the place whence others were fleeing, and steering a direct course, kept the helm straight for the point of danger, so utterly devoid of fear that every movement of the looming portent and every change in its appearance he described and had noted down by his secretary, as soon as his eyes detected it. Already ashes were beginning to fall upon the ships, hotter and in thicker showers as they approached more nearly, with pumice-stones and black flints, charred and cracked by the heat of the flames, while their way was barred by the sudden shoaling of the sea bottom and the litter of the mountain on the shore. He hesitated for a moment whether to turn back, and then, when the helmsman warned him to do so, he exclaimed, 'Fortune favours the bold; try to reach Pomponianus.' The latter was at Stabiae, separated by the whole width of the bay, for the sea there pours in upon a gently rounded and curving shore.

Although the danger was not yet close upon him, it was none the less clearly seen, and it travelled quickly as it came nearer, so Pomponianus had got his baggage together on shipboard, and had determined upon flight, and was waiting for the wind which was blowing on shore to fall. My uncle sailed in with the wind fair behind him, and embraced Pomponianus, who was in a state of fright, comforting and cheering him at the same time. Then in order to calm his friend's fears by showing how composed he was himself, he ordered the servants to carry him to the bath, and, after his ablutions, he sat down and had dinner in the best of spirits, or with that assumption of good spirits which is quite as remarkable as the reality.

In the meantime broad sheets of flame, which rose high in the air, were breaking out in a number of places on Mount Vesuvius and lighting up the sky, and the glare and brightness seemed all the more striking owing to the darkness of the night. My uncle, in order to allay the fear of his companions, kept declaring that the country people in their terror had left their fires burning, and that the conflagration they saw arose from the blazing and empty villas. Then he betook himself to rest and enjoyed a very deep sleep, for his breathing, which, owing to his bulk, was rather heavy and loud, was heard by those who were waiting at the door of his chamber. But by this time the courtyard leading to the room he occupied was so full of ashes and pumice-stones mingled together, and covered to such a depth, that if he had delayed any longer in the bedchamber there would have been no means of escape. So my uncle was aroused, and came out and joined Pomponianus and the rest who had been keeping watch. They held a consultation whether they should remain indoors or wander forth in the open; for the buildings were beginning to shake with the repeated and intensely severe shocks of earthquake, and seemed to be rocking to and fro as though they had been torn from their foundations. Outside again there was danger to be apprehended from the pumice-stones, though these were light and nearly burnt through, and thus, after weighing the two perils, the latter course was determined upon. With my uncle it was a choice of reasons which prevailed, with the rest a choice of fears.

They placed pillows on their heads and secured them with cloths, as a precaution against the falling bodies. Elsewhere the day had dawned by this time, but there it was still night, and the darkness was blacker and thicker than any ordinary night. This, however, they relieved as best they could by a number of torches and other kinds of lights. They decided to make their way to the shore, and to see from the nearest point whether the sea would enable them to put out, but it was still running high and contrary. A sheet was spread on the ground, and on this my uncle lay, and twice he called for a draught of cold water, which he drank. Then the flames, and the smell of sulphur which gave warning of them, scattered the others in flight and roused him. Leaning on two slaves, he rose to his feet and immediately fell down again, owing, as I think, to his breathing being obstructed by the thickness of the fumes and congestion of the stomach, that organ being naturally weak and narrow, and subject to inflammation. When daylight returned – two days after the last day he had seen – his body was found untouched, uninjured, and covered, dressed just as he had been in life. The corpse suggested a person asleep rather than a dead man.

Meanwhile my mother and I were at Misenum. But that is of no consequence for the purposes of history, nor indeed did you express a wish to be told of anything except of my uncle's death. So I will say no more, except to add that I have given you a full account both of the incidents which I myself witnessed and of those narrated to me immediately afterwards, when, as a rule, one gets the truest account of what has happened. You will pick out what you think will answer your purpose best, for to write a letter is a different thing from writing a history, and to write to a friend is not like writing to all and sundry.

Farewell.

Voltaire to M. Tronchin, 24 November 1755

Voltaire was the most famous European of his day, and a master of the art of letter-writing in its golden age. His letters were often copied out for public distribution and read across the continent. Voltaire – real name François-Marie Arouet, born in 1694 – was the polymathic French author of the satirical novel *Candide*, and of poetry, history and essays. He corresponded with monarchs like Frederick the Great and Catherine the Great while he amassed a huge fortune through financial speculation. '*Écrasez l'infâme!*' he often wrote – wipe out superstition, particularly as regards religion. His wit was razor-sharp: 'I disapprove of what you say, but I will defend to the death your right to say it.'

Voltaire initially enjoyed the king's patronage, but soon fell foul of royal censorship and retired to live in splendour at his chateau in Switzerland. His first great love was the clever beauty the Marquise du Châtelet – a mother of three who was also a philosopher and scientist – and then after her death, his own young niece. On All Saints' Day 1755 an earthquake hit Lisbon, killing over thirty thousand, a natural disaster that shocked Europe. Voltaire wrote his *Poem on the Disaster of Lisbon* in response to the destruction. Here in a letter he considers the meaning of such events in a way that seems just as appropriate today.

This is indeed a cruel piece of natural philosophy! We shall find it difficult to discover how the laws of movement operate in such fearful disasters <u>in the best of all possible worlds</u> – where a hundred thousand ants, our neighbours, are crushed in a second on our ant-heaps, half dying undoubtedly in inexpressible agonies, beneath débris from which it was impossible to extricate them, families all over Europe reduced to beggary, and the fortunes of a hundred merchants – Swiss, like yourself – swallowed up in the ruins of Lisbon. What a game of chance human life is! What will the preachers say – especially if the Palace of the Inquisition is left standing! I flatter myself that those reverend fathers, the Inquisitors, will have been crushed just like other people. That ought to teach men not to persecute men: for, while a few sanctimonious humbugs are burning a few fanatics, the earth opens and swallows up all alike. I believe it is our mountains which save us from earthquakes.

Friendship

Captain A.D. Chater to his mother, Christmas 1914

Captain A.D. 'Dougan' Chater, of the 2nd Battalion Gordon Highland-ers, writes this letter home in the hope that the chivalry, decency and friendship shown by both sides in the first Christmas of conflict will overcome the duty to fight and kill. When the Great War started in August 1914, most people presumed it would be over by Christmas. It wasn't, and instead the war deteriorated into the slaughter of trench warfare. But here Chater describes the 'extraordinary sights' of the Christmas Truce of that first year of war. He does not mention the football games that took place between the English and the Germans in other sectors of the Front. Chater was later wounded at the Battle of Neuve Chapelle in March 1915, but survived, married his girlfriend Joy in 1916, and lived until 1974.

Dearest Mother,

I am writing this in the trenches in my 'dug out' – with a wood fire going and plenty of straw. It is rather cosy although it is freezing hard and real Christmas weather.

I think I have seen one of the most extraordinary sights today that anyone has ever seen. About 10 o'clock this morning I was peeping over the parapet when I saw a German waving his arms and presently two of them got out of their trenches and came towards ours. We were just going to fire on them when we saw they had no rifles so one of our men went out to meet them and in about two minutes the ground between the two lines of trenches was swarming with men and officers of both sides, shaking hands and wishing each other a happy Christmas. This continued for about half an hour when most of our men were ordered back to the trenches.

For the rest of the day nobody has fired a shot and men have been wandering about at will on the top of the parapet and carrying straw and fire wood about in the open.

We have also had joint burial parties with a service for some of the dead – some German and some ours – who were lying out between the lines. Some of our officers were taking groups of British and German soldiers. This extraordinary truce has been quite impromptu. There was no previous arrangement and of course it had been decided that there was not to be any cessation of hostilities. I went out myself and shook hands with several of their officers and men. From what I gathered most of them would be as glad to get home again as we should. We have had our pipes playing all day and everyone has been wandering about in the open unmolested but not of course as far as the enemy lines. The truce will probably go on until someone is foolish enough to let off his rifle. We nearly messed it up this afternoon, by one of our fellows letting off his rifle skywards by mistake but they did not seem to notice it so it did not matter. I have been taking advantage of the truce to improve my 'dug out' which I share with D M Bain, the Scotch rugger international – an excellent fellow.

We put on a proper roof this morning and now we have got a tiled fire place and brushwood and straw on the floor. We leave the trenches tomorrow and I shan't be sorry as it is much too cold to be pleasant at nights.

27th. I am writing this back in billets – the same business continues as yesterday and we had another parley with the Germans in the middle. We exchanged cigarettes and autographs and some more people took photos.

I don't know how long it will go on for – I believe it was supposed to stop yesterday but we can hear no firing going on along the front today except a little distant shelling.

We are, at any rate, having another truce on New Year's Day as the Germans want to see how the photos come out! Yesterday was lovely in the morning and I went for several quite long walks about the lines. It is difficult to realise what that means but of course in the ordinary way there is not a sign of life above ground and everyone who puts his head up gets shot at.

It is really very extraordinary that this sort of thing should happen in a war in which there is so much bitterness and ill feeling. The Germans in the front of the line are certainly sportsmen if they are nothing else. Of course I don't suppose it has happened everywhere along the line although I think that indiscriminate fighting has more or less stopped in most places on Christmas Day . . .

Your loving son,
Dougan

Mark Antony to Octavian (later Augustus), c.33 BC

When two friends rule the world, this is the letter they write when they fall out because one of them falls in love with an Egyptian queen.

The heir to the Roman dictator Julius Caesar was his teenage great-nephew Octavian. In 44 BC, Caesar was assassinated. Octavian came to Rome to seek vengeance, forming an alliance with his uncle's top henchman Mark Antony. After destroying the assassins led by Brutus and Cassius, Octavian and Antony divide the Roman world, Octavian ruling Rome and the west while Antony governs the east from Antioch, including Syria and the client kingdom of Egypt. Antony marries Octavian's sister Octavia to cement their alliance.

Egypt, the richest surviving state in Antony's east, is ruled by Cleopatra, heir to the grandest royal dynasty of the ancient world, the Ptolemies, who were Greeks descended from one of Alexander the Great's generals. Now the Mediterranean is dominated by Rome, she needs the favour of the strongman of Rome. Earlier, she had had an affair with Caesar himself, bearing him a son. Now, aged thirty, she meets the bluff and virile soldier Antony, and they fall in love and have children. Together they rule the east with a mixture of Greek style and eastern ritual, promising kingdoms to their children as if it is Antony's personal empire. The Romans sneer at Antony for his showy decadence: Octavian encourages the idea that a Roman imperator under the control of an oriental queen is effete, unmanly, un-Roman. Furious at Octavian's manipulations back in Rome, Antony fires this earthy letter to his ex-friend, mocking the hypocrisy of this well-known womaniser. But Octavian's lovers were Roman, and Antony, isolated in his eastern grandeur with the fascinating Cleopatra, fails to see how dangerous his situation is becoming: he has lost the support of Rome. The two moved towards war: in 31 BC, Octavian defeated Antony and Cleopatra at sea, and the lovers committed suicide. Taking the name Augustus (meaning 'Illustrious'), Octavius then became Rome's first emperor.

What has come over you? Do you object to me screwing Cleopatra? But we are married; and it's not even as if this is anything new – the affair started nine years ago. And what about you? Are you faithful to Livia Drusilla? My congratulations if when this letter arrives you have not been to bed with Tertullia or Terentilla or Rufilla or Salvia Titisenia – or all of them. Does it really matter so much where or with whom one gets it up?

Between Karl Marx and Friedrich Engels, July 1862– November 1864

The letters between Karl Marx and Friedrich Engels are shockingly racist to modern ears but they reveal some of the flaws at the heart of Marxism. Marx and his friend Engels were the creators of an ideology known as Marxism that changed the world. Both born in Prussian territory, Marx was the son of Jewish intellectuals while Engels's father was a wealthy industrialist, a cotton manufacturer. But both were fascinated, horrified and inspired by the cruel inequalities of the capitalist system and the plight of the working class. When they met in 1844 in Paris, Engels, already the author of the The Condition of the Working Class in England, convinced Marx that the working class itself would the engine for a future revolution. Moving between Brussels and Britain, the two cooperated in the creation of a secret revolutionary movement, the League of the Just that became the Communist League, and wrote their seminal text The Communist Manifesto with its famed opening sentence: 'The history of all hitherto existing society is the history of class struggles.' In this and Marx's future work Das Kapital, the two argued that the capitalist exploitation of the working class would lead to a class struggle and ultimately a revolution by the oppressed proletariat, and a new era of equality and communism in which the state, no longer necessary, would wither away.

Marx and Engels' most exciting moments were during the feverish months of the 1848 Revolutions but when the revolutions were crushed they retreated to Britain. Engels helped run his family companies and paid Marx's expenses. In their long correspondence, Marx called himself 'the Moor' (for his swarthiness) while Engels was 'the General'. While Engels lived with two sisters, who in turn were his mistresses, Marx was married to a well-connected and longsuffering Prussian baroness Jenny von Westphalen who, while living in increasing poverty in Soho and Primrose Hill in London, bore him seven children, four of whom died young. Meanwhile Marx was having adulterous affairs with their housekeeper Helene Demuth with whom he had a son.

Engels was jovial, social and pleasure-loving; Marx was brooding, selfish and intolerant but also enjoyed gossip and dancing. But both men were wildly jealous of their fellow socialist, Ferdinand Lassalle, who was in many ways what they wished to be: a political star, bon vivant, brilliant showman and brazen lover who founded his own organization and was supported financially by his mistress Countess von Hatzfeldt. Lassalle was so charismatic and influential that the reactionary minister Count Bismarck consulted him secretly.

Lassalle recognized Marx's talent and originality, helping him to get his work published, but both Marx and Engels maliciously repaid the favour with an endless stream of racist epithets from 'stupid Yid' to 'Jewboy' and the even more racist 'Nigger'. The first letter quoted here reveals their weirdly antisemitic and racist analysis of Lassalle but two years later, Lassalle embarked on an affair with a young woman engaged to a Wallachian prince whom he foolishly challenged to a duel. Lassalle was killed. Marx and Engels were astonished by the rise and fall of this flamboyant meteor – but Engels' reflections on Lassalle's intellectual and sexual power are particularly striking: 'she didn't want his beautiful mind but his Jewish cock.'

London, 30 July 1862

Dear Engels,

From the enclosed scraps you'll see up to a point how I am bothered. The landlord meanwhile has been pacified, he has to get 25£. The piano man, who is paid in instalments for the piano, was to have received 6£ on the last day of June, and is a very rude lout. I have tax demands for 6£ in the house. That school muck of about 10£ I have fortunately paid since I'm doing all I can to spare the children direct humiliation. I've paid the butcher 6£ (and this was my total quarterly income from Presse!) but the blighter is pestering me again, not to mention the baker, the teagrocer, the greengrocer and whatever the names of those devils are.

That Jewish nigger Lassalle, who is fortunately leaving at the end of this week, has happily again lost 5,000 Taler in a mis-speculation. The blighter would sooner fling his money into the mud than lend it to a 'friend', even if interest as well as capital were guaranteed him. At the same time he proceeds from the view that he has to live as a Jewish baron or baronized (probably by the Countess) Jew. Would you believe it that the blighter, who is aware of the business with America, etc., i.e. is aware of the crisis in which I find myself, had the impertinence to ask me if I wanted to hand one of my daughters over to the Hatzfeldt woman as 'companion' and whether he himself should obtain for me Gerstenberg's [sic] protection! The fellow cost me a lot of time and, so the oaf suggested, since at the moment I had 'no business' but was engaged merely on 'theoretical work', I might just as well kill time with him! In order to observe a certain social propriety vis-à-vis the fellow my wife had to take anything that was not actually screwed down to the pawnshop!

If I weren't in this hideous position, and if the parvenu's slapping of his money-bag did not irritate me so, I would have been royally amused. Since I saw him a year ago he has become totally mad. His stay in Zurich (with Rüstow, Herwegh, etc.) and his subsequent journey, and finally his 'Herr Julian Schmidt', etc., have completely gone to his head. He is now by general agreement not only the greatest scholar, the most profound thinker, the most inspired researcher, etc., but also Don Juan and a revolutionary Cardinal Richelieu. And with it that unceasing babbling in his squeaking falsetto voice, his unaesthetically demonstrative movement, his didactic tone! . . .

. . . Lasalle was most furious about me and wife for poking fun at his plans, poking fun at him as an 'enlightened Bonapartist', etc. He screamed, raved, jumped about and in the end utterly convinced himself that I am too 'abstract' to understand politics.

. . . As I said, in different circumstances (and if he had not got into the way of my work) the blighter would have royally amused me.

Add to this the immoderate beastlike eating and the randy lust of this 'idealist'.

It is now perfectly clear to me that, as testified also by his cranial formation and hair growth, he is descended from the negroes who joined Moses's exodus from Egypt (unless his paternal mother or grandmother was crossed with a nigger).

Well, this combination of Jewish and Germanic stock with the negroid base substance is bound to yield a strange product. The fellow's importunity is also nigger-like. . . .

Yours, K.M.

London, 2 September 1864

Dear Frederick,

Yesterday afternoon I received the letter from Freiligrath copies below, from which you will see that Lassalle was critically wounded in a duel in Geneva. I went to see Freiligrath the same evening. But he had not received any later telegrams. . . .

Yours, K.M.

Manchester, 4 September 1864

Dear Moor,

Your telegram arrived yesterday, even before I opened your letter since all kinds of business immediately took up my time. You may as well imagine the news surprised me. Whatever else Lassalle may have been, as a person, as a literary man, as a scholar – politically he was certainly one of the most significant fellows in Germany. To us at present he was a very uncertain friend, in future a fairly certain enemy, but be that as it may – it does hit one hard to see Germany finishing off all reasonably good people of the extremist party. What jubilation will reign now among the manufacturers and among those progressive pigs. Lassalle after all was the only chap in Germany itself of whom they were afraid.

But what a strange way to lose one's life: to fall seriously in love with the daughter of a Bavarian envoy – that would-be Don Juan – to want to marry her, to clash with a retired rival, who moreover is a Wallachian cheat, and to be shot dead by him. That could only happen to Lassalle, given his

strange mixture of frivolity and sentimentality, Jewishness
and cavalier posturing that was his and his alone. How
could a political man like him shoot it out with a Wallachian
adventurer!

. . .

Yours, F.E.

London, 7 September 1864

Dear Frederick,

Lassalle's disaster has been damnably on my mind these
days. When all is said and done, he was one of the old
stock and the enemy of our enemies. Besides, the thing
came as such a surprise that it is hard to believe that such
a boisterous, stirring, pushing person is now dead as a
door-nail and has to keep utterly silent. As for the ostensible
occasion for his death, you are quite right. It is another
of the many tactless actions he has committed in his life.
With all that I am sorry that during the past few years our
relationship was troubled, albeit through his fault. . . .

Yours, K.M.

Manchester, 7 November 1864

Dear Moor,

. . . Evidently Lassalle's undoing was that he did not
immediately fling Helene von Dönniges on to the bed in
the guest-house and have a good go at her; she didn't want
his beautiful mind but his Jewish cock. It's simply one more
affair that could only have happened to Lassalle. That *he*
forced the Wallachian to duel is doubly crazy. . . .

Yours, F.E.

Franklin D. Roosevelt to Winston Churchill, 11 September 1939

The first letter of the friendship that would hold the West.

On 3 September 1939, Britain declared war on Germany, which had invaded Poland. The Second World War had begun. Churchill returned to the cabinet as First Lord of the Admiralty, the job he had held in 1914, the start of the First World War. A few days later, he receives this letter from the US President Franklin Roosevelt who had served in a similar job – Assistant Secretary of the Navy, during the same war. They had met passingly twenty years earlier, and in 1933 when Roosevelt won the presidential election Churchill had sent him a copy of his biography of the Duke of Marlborough, but he had not acknowledged it. Now he does so – and opens up a secret channel with Churchill. Although Roosevelt mentions Prime Minister Neville Chamberlain in this letter, it is a formality since both men know how inept Chamberlain has been in appeasing Hitler. Roosevelt is betting that Churchill is the coming man. When he became Prime Minister eight months later, their alliance would be decisive.

My dear Churchill,

It is because you and I occupied similar positions in the [first] world war that I want you to know how glad I am that you are back again in the Admiralty. Your problems are, I realize, complicated by new factors, but the essential is not very different. What I want you and the Prime Minister to know is that I shall at all times welcome it if you will keep me in touch personally with anything you want me to know about. You can always send sealed letters through your pouch or my pouch.

I am glad you did the Marlborough volumes before this thing started – and I much enjoyed reading them.

With my sincere regards,

Faithfully yours,

Franklin D. Roosevelt

Adolf Hitler to Benito Mussolini, 21 June 1941

A letter from Hitler to his closest friend in international affairs at the height of his power. It is written the night before he invades Soviet Russia, the hubristic act that ultimately led to the downfall of the Third Reich. Hitler had once admired Benito Mussolini, Fascist dictator of Italy since 1922, basing many of his tactics, even the creation of his own Nazi party, on Italian fascism. But by 1941 Hitler saw him as a preposterous blowhard, while the Italian Duce regarded Hitler as a coarse and dangerous tyrant. But Hitler was now the senior partner. The letter is filled with half-truths: he has actually been planning the Russian invasion for many months (hiding it from Mussolini); and his swaggering delusions and brutal miscalculations are starkly revealed in the extraordinary way he boasts of a decision that would launch the most barbarous war in human history and cost the lives of over thirty million people. This is the way he sees the world when he believes no one can stop him.

21 June 1941

Duce!

I am writing this letter to you at a moment when months of anxious deliberation and continuous nerve-racking waiting are ending in the hardest decision of my life. I believe – after seeing the latest Russian situation map and after appraisal of numerous other reports – that I cannot take the responsibility for waiting longer, and above all, I believe that there is no other way of obviating this danger – unless it be further waiting, which, however, would necessarily lead to disaster in this or the next year at the latest.

The situation: England has lost this war. With the right of the drowning person, she grasps at every straw which, in her imagination, might serve as a sheet anchor. Nevertheless, some of her hopes are naturally not without a certain logic. England has thus far always conducted her wars with help from the Continent. The destruction of France – fact, the elimination of all west-European positions – directing the glances of the British warmongers continually to the place from which they tried to start the war: to Soviet Russia.

Both countries, Soviet Russia and England, are equally interested in a Europe fallen into ruin, rendered prostrate by a long war. Behind these two countries stands the North American Union goading them on and watchfully waiting. Since the liquidation of Poland, there is evident in Soviet Russia a consistent trend, which, even if cleverly and cautiously, is nevertheless reverting firmly to the old Bolshevist tendency to expansion of the Soviet State. The prolongation of the war necessary for this purpose is to be achieved by tying up German forces in the East, so that – particularly in the air – the German Command can no longer vouch for a large-scale attack in the West. I declared to you only recently, Duce, that it was precisely the success of the experiment in Crete that demonstrated how necessary it is to make use of every single airplane in the much greater project against England. It may well happen that in this decisive battle we would win with a superiority of only a few squadrons. I shall not hesitate a moment to undertake such a responsibility if, aside from all other conditions, I at least possess the one certainty that I will not then suddenly be attacked or even threatened from the East. The concentration of Russian forces – I had General Jodl submit the most recent map to your Attaché here, General Maras – is tremendous. Really, all available Russian forces are at our border. Moreover, since the approach of warm weather, work has been proceeding on numerous defenses. If circumstances should give me cause to employ the German air force against England, there is a danger that Russia will then begin its strategy of extortion in the South and North, to which I would have to yield in silence, simply from a feeling of air inferiority. It would, above all, not then be possible for me without adequate support from an air force, to attack the Russian fortifications with the divisions stationed in the East. If I do not wish to expose myself to this danger, then perhaps the whole year of 1941 will go by without any change in the general situation. On the contrary. England will be all the less ready for peace, for it will be able to pin its hopes on the Russian partner. Indeed, this hope must naturally even grow with the progress in preparedness of the Russian armed forces. And behind this is the mass delivery of war material from America which they hope to get in 1942.

Aside from this, Duce, it is not even certain whether I shall have this time, for with so gigantic a concentration of forces on both sides – for I also was compelled to place more and more armored units on the eastern border, also to call Finland's and Romania's attention to the danger – there is the possibility that the shooting will start spontaneously at any moment. A withdrawal on my part would, however, entail a serious loss of prestige for us. This would be particularly unpleasant in its possible effect on Japan. I have, therefore, after constantly racking my brains, finally reached the decision to cut the noose before it can be drawn tight. I believe, Duce, that I am hereby rendering probably the best possible service to our joint conduct of the war this year. For my overall view is now as follows:

1. France is, as ever, not to be trusted. Absolute surety that North Africa will not suddenly desert does not exist.
2. North Africa itself, insofar as your colonies, Duce, are concerned, is probably out of danger until autumn. I assume that the British, in their last attack, wanted to relieve Tobruk. I do not believe they will soon be in a position to repeat this.
3. Spain is irresolute and – I am afraid – will take sides only

when the outcome of the war is decided.

4. In Syria, French resistance can hardly be maintained permanently either with or without our help.

5. An attack on Egypt before autumn is out of the question altogether. I consider it necessary, however, taking into account the whole situation, to give thought to the development of an operational unit in Tripoli itself which can, if necessary, also be launched against the West. Of course, Duce, the strictest silence must be maintained with regard to these ideas, for otherwise we cannot expect France to continue to grant permission to use its ports for the transportation of arms and munitions.

6. Whether or not America enters the war is a matter of indifference, inasmuch as she supports our opponent with all the power she is able to mobilize.

7. The situation in England itself is bad; the provision of food and raw materials is growing steadily more difficult. The martial spirit to make war, after all, lives only on hopes. These hopes are based solely on two assumptions: Russia and America. We have no chance of eliminating America. But it does lie in our power to exclude Russia. The elimination of Russia means, at the same time, a tremendous relief for Japan in East Asia, and thereby the possibility of a much stronger threat to American activities through Japanese intervention.

I have decided under these circumstances as I already mentioned, to put an end to the hypocritical performance in the Kremlin. I assume, that is to say, I am convinced, that Finland, and likewise Romania, will forthwith take part in this conflict, which will ultimately free Europe, for the future also, of a great danger. General Maras informed us that you, Duce, wish also to make available at least one corps. If you have that intention, Duce – which I naturally accept with a heart filled with gratitude – the time for carrying it out will still be sufficiently long, for in this immense theatre of war the troops cannot be assembled at all points at the same time anyway. You, Duce, can give the decisive aid, however, by strengthening your forces in North Africa, also, if possible, looking from Tripoli toward the West, by proceeding further to build up a group which, though it be small at first, can march into France in case of a French violation of the treaty; and finally, by carrying the air war and, so far as it is possible, the submarine war, in intensified degree, into the Mediterranean.

So far as the security of the territories in the West is concerned, from Norway to and including France, we are strong enough there – so far as army troops are concerned – to meet any eventuality with lightning speed. So far as air war on England is concerned, we shall, for a time remain on the defensive, – but this does not mean that we might be incapable of countering British attacks on Germany; on the contrary, we shall, if necessary, be in a position to start ruthless bombing attacks on British home territory. Our fighter defence, too, will be adequate. It consists of the best squadrons that we have.

As far as the war in the East is concerned, Duce, it will surely be difficult, but I do not entertain a second's doubt as to its great success. I hope, above all, that it will then be possible for us to secure a common food-supply base in the Ukraine for some time to come, which will furnish us such additional supplies as we may need in the future. I may state at this point, however, that, as far as we can tell now, this year's German harvest promises to be a very good one. It is conceivable that Russia will try to destroy the Romanian oil region. We have built up a defence that will – or so I think – prevent the worst. Moreover, it is the duty of our armies to eliminate this threat as rapidly as possible.

I waited until this moment, Duce, to send you this information, it is because the final decision itself will not be made until 7 o'clock tonight. I earnestly beg you, therefore, to refrain, above all, from making any explanation to your Ambassador at Moscow, for there is no absolute guarantee that our coded reports cannot be decoded. I, too, shall wait until the last moment to have my own Ambassador informed of the decisions reached.

The material that I now contemplate publishing gradually, is so exhaustive that the world will have more occasion to wonder at our forbearance than at our decision, except for that part of the world which opposes us on principle and for which, therefore, arguments are of use.

Whatever may now come, Duce, our situation cannot become worse as a result of this step; it can only improve. Even if I should be obliged at the end of this year to leave 60 or 70 divisions in Russia, that is only a fraction of the forces that I am now continually using on the eastern front. Should England nevertheless not draw any conclusions from the hard facts that present themselves, then we can, with our rear secured, apply ourselves with increased strength to the dispatching of our opponent. I can promise you, Duce, that what lies in our German power, will be done.

Any desires, suggestions, and assistance of which you, Duce, wish to inform me in the contingency before us, I would request that you either communicate to me personally or have them agreed upon directly by our military authorities.

In conclusion, let me say one more thing, Duce. Since I struggled through to this decision, I again feel spiritually free. The partnership with the Soviet Union, in spite of the complete sincerity of the efforts to bring about a final conciliation, was nevertheless often very irksome to me, for in some way or other it seemed to me to be a break with my whole origin, my concepts, and my former obligations. I am happy now to be relieved of these mental agonies.

With hearty and comradely greetings,
Your ADOLF HITLER

Between Prince Potemkin and Catherine the Great, c.1774

How to settle a row – by letter (or email). Catherine the Great and Prince Potemkin, her brilliant lover and minister, were wildly in love with each other but he was restless at being at her beck and call: he wanted to be a chief minister, a commander, an empire-builder.

After an argument, he calmly apologises for his tempestuous nature and then on the same piece of paper she answers his complaints in this double letter, concluding 'End of quarrel'. It is not unlike an email thread. But even this civilised negotiation did not solve the problem, until she secretly married him and agreed that they would continue ruling like husband and wife – except both would be allowed their own, younger, lovers. The strange arrangement worked, and they ruled Russia together with great success for almost twenty years, ending only with Potemkin's death in 1791. She survived another five years but she never got over the prince: 'There'll never another Potemkin,' she often said.

Potemkin	Catherine
Let me my love say this	I allow it.
Which will, I hope, end our argument.	The sooner the better.
Don't be surprised I am Disturbed by our love.	Don't be disturbed.
Not only have you showered me With good deeds, You have placed me in your Heart. I want to be There alone, and above everyone else	You are there firmly & strongly & will remain there.
Because no one has ever loved you so much	I see it and believe it.
And I have been made by your hands	Happy to do so.
That you should be happy in being good To me;	It will be my greatest pleasure.
That you should find rest from the Great labours arising from your high Station in thinking of my comfort.	Of course.
Amen.	Give rest to our thoughts and let our feelings act freely. They are most tender and will find the best way. End of quarrel. Amen.

Folly

Georg von Hülsen to Emil von Görtz, 1892

The courtiers of Kaiser Wilhelm II, the leader of the German empire, tried hard, year after year, to provide the sort of crass entertainment their monarch craved. During his long reign – 1888 to 1918 – his political and diplomatic antics not only appalled his own officials and ministers, but also alarmed the chancelleries of Europe, thereby raising the tensions that led to the First World War.

Bombastic, brutish and boastful, narcissistic and vain, nationalistic, inconsistent and impulsive, obsessed with power and claiming credit for everything while operating under the burdens of a mountainous ego and matching inferiority complex, Wilhelm is in some ways a familiar modern character. He also possessed an extremely childish sense of humour. He delighted in cutting his generals' braces off with his penknife, or chasing old colonels to bed, or rolling them downhill. Cross-dressing, sausages and bare bottoms were also royal favourites. As we see in this extract from a letter sent before a hunt in 1892, close friend Count 'Em' von Görtz knows exactly what pranks will please the kaiser, planning it with courtier Georg von Hülsen. Their games could go wrong. In 1908, Dietrich von Hülsen, Georg's brother, danced for the kaiser in full ballerina costume, complete with tutu, feather boa and satin pumps – until he fell down dead of a heart attack. Such were the entertainments of the most powerful man in the world: 'I can already see H.M. [His Majesty] laughing . . .'

You must be paraded by me as a circus poodle! – That will 'hit' like nothing else. Just think: behind shaved [tights], in front long bangs out of black or white wool, at the back under a genuine poodle tail a marked rectal opening and, when you beg, in front a fig-leaf. Just think how wonderful when you bark, howl to music, shoot off a pistol or do other tricks. It is simply splendid!! . . . In my mind's eye I can already see H.M. [His Majesty] laughing with us . . . I am applying myself with real relish to this 'work' in order to forget that my beloved sister – the dearest thing I have on earth – is at this moment dying in Breslau . . . I feel like the clown in [Ludwig] Knaus's picture 'Behind the Scenes'. No matter! – H.M. shall be satisfied!

The Marquis de Sade 'to the stupid villains who torment me', 1783

A letter of sadism. The philosopher, libertine and sexual deviant, Donatien, Marquis de Sade spent nearly half of his life in prisons or mental asylums, accused of sodomy and perversion. As a boy, it was a schoolmaster's thrashing that ignited a fascination with pain and pleasure – and the connection between the two. Abandoned by his aristocratic family, his playful and cruel whims were indulged by servants. He served in the army while he embarked on a spree of seductions, beatings, torments and sodomy with women and men of all ages, some of them distastefully young. Promoted to colonel during the Seven Years War, he married a magistrate's daughter Renée-Pélagie de Montreuil with whom he had three children. Their marriage soon failed, and when he was faced with a blizzard of denunciations for perversion that almost led to his execution, his mother-in-law Mme de Montreuil won him some protection from the law by procuring a *lettre de cachet*, a royal letter that allowed de Sade to be confined indefinitely without trial.

In prison Sade wrote his brilliant but demented and obscene novels, such as *Justine*, which were as manaically brazen and violently ingenuous as his orgies. Confined to the Château de Vincennes between 1777 and 1784, de Sade amuses himself by writing this vicious letter to his tormentors, especially 'the strumpet', his mother-in-law, for whom he devises sadistic punishments. When the Revolution came, de Sade was in the Bastille writing *120 Days of Sodom* and encouraged the crowd to attack the fortress, but he was removed to a lunatic asylum before it fell to the revolutionaries. Nonetheless he was liberated and joined the Revolution, serving as a high official while enjoying his freedoms until he opposed Robespierre's Terror, which led to his arrest. He was lucky not to be guillotined. Napoleon Bonaparte returned him to the asylum, and while there he seduced the fourteen-year-old daughter of an employee. He died in 1814.

Vincennes,

Vile minions of the tunny-fish vendors of Aix, low and infamous servants of torturers, invent then for my torment tortures from which at least some good may result. What is the effect of the inaction in which your spiritual purblindness keeps me except to curse and lacerate the unworthy procuress who so meanly contrived to sell me to you? Since I can neither read nor write any longer, this is the hundred and eleventh torture which I am inventing for her. This morning as I suffered I saw her, the strumpet, I saw her flayed alive, dragged over thistles and then thrown into a barrel of vinegar. And I said to her:

Execrable creature that is for selling your son-in-law to the torturers!

Take that, you procuress, for hiring out your two daughters!

Take that for having ruined and dishonoured your son-in-law!

Take that for making him hate the children for whose sake supposedly you sacrifice him!

Take that for having wrecked the best years of his life when it rested with you alone to help him after his sentence!

Take that for having preferred the vile and detestable offspring of your daughter to him!

Take that for all the wickedness with which you overwhelmed him for thirteen years, to make him pay for your stupidities!

And I increased her tortures, and insulted her in her pain and forgot mine.

My pen falls from my hand. I must suffer.

Adieu, torturers, I must curse you.

Between Empress Alexandra and Nicholas II, 1916

A wife writes to her beloved husband at the Front during the First World War, in quaint upper-class English full of nicknames like Agooweeone (him) and Wify and Sunny (her). But this is no ordinary couple, and it is a letter that shows why Russia is just weeks from the Revolution. This is Tsarina Alexandra in the country's capital, Petrograd, writing to her husband Nicholas II who is at military headquarters. She urges Nicholas to be 'the master', like Peter the Great and Ivan the Terrible before him. Her advice is backed by the divine authority of 'our Friend' Rasputin, who she sees as the successor of the couple's earlier healer, a charlatan 'doctor' named Monsieur Philippe. Obsessed with autocracy, halting democracy and judging every political or military decision by whether it was good or bad for Rasputin, she is a catastrophic influence, aggressively proposing political appointments like her candidate for Interior Minister, Alexander Protopopov, a half-mad cocaine-addicted syphilitic. She boasts she is the most powerful woman in Russia since Catherine the Great. Her only redeeming feature is her devotion to her family and 'Nicky' himself, whose caresses she longs for – as he does hers.

Alexandra to Nicholas, 14 December 1916

7 of frost and thick snow. Scarcely slept this night again, remaining till luncheon in bed as all aches still and have a slight chill. Such loving thanks for your dear letter.

Be Peter the Great, Ivan the Terrible, Emperor Paul – crush them all under you – now don't you laugh, naughty one.

I really cannot understand. I am but a woman, but my
soul and brain tell me it would be the saving of Russia – they
sin far worse than anything the Sukhomlinovs ever did.
Forbid Brusilov etc. when they come to touch any political
subjects, fool, who wants responsible cabinet.

Remember even M. Philippe said one dare not give
constitution, as it would be your and Russia's ruin, and all
true Russians say the same.

Months ago I told [Premier] Sturmer about Shvedov to be
a member of Council of the Empire to have them and good
Maklokov in they will stand bravely for us. I know I worry
you – ah, would I not far, far rather only write letters of
love, tenderness and caresses of which my heart is so full –
but my duty as wife and mother and Russia's mother obliges
me to say all to you – blessed by our Friend.

Sweetheart, sunshine of my life, if in battle you had to
meet the enemy, you would never waver and go forth like
a lion – be it now in the battle against the small handful of
brutes and republicans.

Be the Master, and all will bow down to you. Do you
think I should fear, ah no – today I have had an officer
cleared out from [their daughters] Maria's and Anastasia's
hospital, because he allowed himself to mock at our journey,
pretending Protopopov brought the people to receive us so
well; the Doctors who heard it raged – you see Sunny in her
small things is energetic and in big ones as much as you wish
– we have been placed by God on a throne and we must
keep it firm and give it over to our son untouched – if you
keep that in mind you will remember to be the Sovereign –
and how much easier for an autocratic sovereign than one
who has sworn the Constitution.

Beloved One, listen to me, yes, you know your old true
girly. 'Do not fear,' the old woman said and therefore I write
without fear to me agooweeone. Now the girlies want their

tea, they came frozen back from their drive – I kiss you and hold you tightly clasped to my breast, caress you, love you, long for you, can't sleep without you – bless you.

Ever your very Own
Wify

Nicholas's replies to Alexandra are equally a mix of misguided arrogance and intimate sentimentality. In this earlier letter he dreams of making love to her again – using the nickname 'Boysy' for his sex: in her letters she calls hers 'Lady'. His loathing of Miechen, wife of his cousin Vladimir, reveals the growing feud with the rest of the Romanov family.

Nicholas to Alexandra, 16 June 1916

My own darling Wify,

Today the messenger is a little late, probably on account of new movements of troops fr north to south. I send you a telegram which [their son, Tsarevich] Aleksei got fr his regiment. Again good news thank God fr Lechitsky! Yesterday his army made 221 officers & 10,200 men prisoners! So many new hands working in our fields & manufact.[ories]. Miechen [Grand Duchess Maria Pavlovna] wrote me a cold letter asking me why I have not approved the polozhenie [Regulation]? I sent it through Alekseev to the Verkh. Soviet. Perhaps you will let Ilin [president of the Russian Red Cross] know that they are to look at it though [sic] & send me their opinion. She is really insufferable – if I have time, I shall answer her sharply. – We have finished lunch & on coming up to my room I found your dear letter No. 520 . . . How I miss your sweet kisses! Yes, beloved One, you know how to give them! Oh, how naughtily! Boysy hops from remembrances. It is very hot & now a few drops of rain fell out of an isolated cloud. I hope to bathe in the river higher up while Aleksei runs about with naked legs. Did he describe to you how the small peasant boys play all sorts of games before us? Now, my precious Darling, I must end. God bless you & the girlies.

With many fond kisses ever your own <u>Nicky</u>.

Decency

Maria Theresa to Marie Antoinette, 30 July 1775

No child enjoys a strict telling-off from their mother, especially on the subjects of manners and morality. Here Empress Maria Theresa scolds her daughter Marie Antoinette, queen of France, for her high-handed rudeness to diplomats and ministers and for running around with flirtatious flatterers while ignoring her dull, weak husband King Louis XVI. The mother is fifty-eight, the daughter nineteen. Maria Theresa has struggled through incessant wars to keep her vast empire together since she inherited it at the age of twenty-three. Then, thirty years later, in 1756, she has pulled a diplomatic coup by marrying her pretty daughter to the king of France. It is clear that the mother glimpses something so dangerous in her daughter that she foresees catastrophe. Maria Theresa would die in 1780; she never saw the 'misfortune' she had feared – the French Revolution and the execution of her daughter.

Madame my dear daughter

I cannot hide from you that a letter you sent to [Minister] Rosenberg upset me most dreadfully. What style! What frivolity! Where is the good and generous heart of the Archduchess Antoinette? I see only intrigue, vulgar spite, delight in mockery and persecution. An intrigue which would do very well for a Pompadour or a Dubarry, but never for a queen, a great princess, still less a princess kindly and good of the house of Lorraine and Austria. All the winter long I have trembled at the thought of your too easy success and the flatterers surrounding you, while you have thrown yourself into a life of pleasure and preposterous display. This chasing from pleasure to pleasure without the king, and knowing that he takes no joy in it and only goes with you or lets you do what you want out of sheer good nature, has made me write before to express my fears. I see now from this letter that these were all too well justified . . .

Your luck can all too easily change, and by your own fault you may well find yourself plunged into deepest misery. That is the result of your terrible dissipation which prevents your being assiduous about anything serious. What have you read? And after that you dare to opine on the greatest State matters, on the choice of ministers? What does the Abbé do? And Mercy? You dislike them because of behaving like low flatterers they want you to be happy and do not take advantage of your weaknesses. One day you will recognise the truth of this, but then it will be too late. I hope I shall not survive until misfortune overtakes you, and I pray to God to end my days quickly, since I am no longer of any use to you, and I could not bear to lose my dear child or see her unhappy, whom I shall love tenderly until I die.

Mahatma Gandhi to Hitler, 24 December 1940

This letter is the ultimate clash of seraphic decency and diabolical evil. At the end of 1940, with the Nazi empire at its height, Europe conquered, Germany apparently invincible, Hitler receives a letter from his diametric opposite, Mahatma Gandhi, who is actively involved in attempting to eject the British from India. Gandhi campaigned against any Indian participation in the war, arguing that his country could not be involved in a conflict over freedom when such a right was denied to India itself. (Nonetheless two and a half million of his countrymen joined the Allied forces.)

The seventy-one-year-old Indian activist had tried in 1939 to counsel Hitler against war, and now appeals to the Führer's better nature by reminding him of his own struggles against British imperialism. He writes from his ashram in Sevagram in Maharashtra, where he lives with his wife and their four children. The letter is as futile as it is admirable. Hitler never replies, going on to perpetrate the Holocaust, invade Russia, and commit suicide in the ruins of Berlin. Gandhi's campaign was successful, leading the British to grant India (and Pakistan) independence. Soon afterwards, Gandhi was assassinated by a fanatical Hindu gunman.

December 24, 1940

DEAR FRIEND,

That I address you as a friend is no formality. I own no foes. My business in life has been for the past 33 years to enlist the friendship of the whole of humanity by befriending mankind, irrespective of race, colour or creed.

I hope you will have the time and desire to know how a good portion of humanity who have been living under the influence of that doctrine of universal friendship view your action. We have no doubt about your bravery or devotion to your fatherland, nor do we believe that you are the monster described by your opponents. But your own writings and pronouncements and those of your friends and admirers leave no room for doubt that many of your acts are monstrous and unbecoming of human dignity, especially in the estimation of men like me who believe in universal friendliness. Such are your humiliation of Czechoslovakia, the rape of Poland and the swallowing of Denmark. I am aware that your view of life regards such spoliations as virtuous acts. But we have been taught from childhood to regard them as acts degrading humanity. Hence we cannot possibly wish success to your arms.

But ours is a unique position. We resist British Imperialism no less than Nazism. If there is a difference, it is in degree. One-fifth of the human race has been brought under the British heel by means that will not bear scrutiny. Our resistance to it does not mean harm to the British people. We seek to convert them, not to defeat them on the battle-field. Ours is an unarmed revolt against the British rule. But whether we convert them or not, we are determined to make their rule impossible by non-violent non-co-operation. It is a method in its nature indefensible. It is based on the knowledge that no spoliator can compass his end without a certain degree of co-operation, willing or compulsory, of the victim. Our rulers may have our land and bodies but not our souls . . .

We know what the British heel means for us and the non-European races of the world. But we would never wish to end the British rule with German aid. We have found in non-violence a force which, if organized, can without doubt match itself against a combination of all the most violent forces in the world. In non-violent technique, as I have said, there is no such thing as defeat. It is all 'do or die' without killing or hurting. It can be used practically without money and obviously without the aid of science or destruction which you have brought to such perfection. It is a marvel to me that you do not see that it is nobody's monopoly. If not the British, some other power will certainly improve upon your method and beat you with your own weapon. You are leaving no legacy to your people of which they would feel proud. They cannot take pride in a recital of cruel deed, however skilfully planned. I, therefore, appeal to you in the name of humanity to stop the war . . .

You know that not long ago I made an appeal to every Briton to accept my method of non-violent resistance. I did it because the British know me as a friend though a rebel. I am a stranger to you and your people. I have not the courage to make to you the appeal I made to every Briton. Not that it would not apply to you with the same force as to the British. But my present proposal is much simpler because much more practical and familiar.

During this season when the hearts of the peoples of Europe yearn for peace, we have suspended even our own peaceful struggle. Is it too much to ask you to make an effort for peace during a time which may mean nothing to you personally but which must mean much to the millions of Europeans whose dumb cry for peace I hear, for my ears are attended to hearing the dumb millions?

I am,

Your sincere friend,

M. K. GANDHI

Abraham Lincoln to Ulysses S. Grant, 13 July 1863

Here President Abraham Lincoln congratulates General Grant whole-heartedly for an important victory during the American Civil War – the capture of Vicksburg, Mississippi – and, remarkably, apologises for getting it completely wrong himself. A masterful letter-writer, Lincoln is famed for his clarity of language, whether political or personal. In a letter of 22 August 1862 he states his real priorities in the conflict: 'I would save the Union. I would save it the shortest way ... What I do about slavery and the colored race I do because I believe it helps save the Union ...'

But he also had a sense of fun: when an eleven-year-old girl named Grace Bedell wrote to advise him to grow more presidential whiskers, Lincoln replied on 19 October 1860: 'My dear little Miss ... As for whiskers, having never worn any, do you not think people would call it a piece of silly affectation if I were to begin now? Your very sincere well wisher A. Lincoln.'

However, this letter is significant strategically and because of what it reveals about Lincoln's character. It means he has finally found a victorious general: he promoted Grant to commanding general and Grant went on to be elected president. It also highlights Lincoln's magnanimity and his confidence in his own gifts. Such humility is rare among bosses of all kinds but especially among politicians.

My dear General

I do not remember that you and I ever met personally. I

write this now as a grateful acknowledgment for the almost inestimable service you have done the country. I wish to say a word further. When you first reached the vicinity of Vicksburg, I thought you should do, what you finally did – march the troops across the neck, run the batteries with the transports, and thus go below; and I never had any faith, except a general hope that you knew better than I, that the Yazoo Pass expedition, and the like, could succeed. When you got below, and took Port-Gibson, Grand Gulf, and vicinity, I thought you should go down the river and join Gen. Banks; and when you turned Northward East of the Big Black, I feared it was a mistake. I now wish to make the personal acknowledgment that you were right, and I was wrong.

Yours very truly
A. Lincoln

John Profumo to Harold Macmillan, 5 June 1963

There is the sin and there is the cover-up. Often the cover-up is worse. This letter of truth and confession ends an era. In 1961 John Profumo, Secretary of State for War in Harold Macmillan's government, admired a beautiful model and demi-mondaine, Christine Keeler, bathing in the pool at Cliveden, the country house of Viscount Astor – and began an affair with her. At the same time she was having an affair with a KGB spy, Soviet naval attaché, Yevgeni Ivanov. Profumo, who was married, denied any 'impropriety' to the Prime Minister and Parliament. But when the truth is exposed he is forced to write this letter to Macmillan. The 'Profumo affair' fatally damages not just the Conservative government but also the old-fashioned public-school Establishment. Macmillan retires, Labour win the next election, and Profumo devotes the rest of his life to charity.

Dear Prime Minister,

You will recollect that on 22 March, following certain allegations made in Parliament, I made a personal statement. At the time the rumour had charged me with assisting in the disappearance of a witness and with being involved in some possible breach of security.

So serious were these charges that I allowed myself to think that my personal association with that witness, which had also been the subject of rumour, was by comparison of minor importance only. In my statement I said there had been no impropriety in this association. To my very deep regret I have to admit that this was not true, and that I misled you and my colleagues and the House.

I ask you to understand that I did this to protect, as I thought, my wife and family, who were misled, as were my professional advisers.

I have come to realise that, by this deception, I have been guilty of a grave misdemeanour and despite the fact that there is no truth whatsoever in the other charges, I cannot remain a member of your Administration, nor of the House of Commons.

I cannot tell you of my deep remorse for the embarrassment I have caused you, to my colleagues in the Government, to my constituents, and to the Party which I have served for the past twenty-five years.

Yours sincerely,
Jack Profumo

Jacqueline Kennedy to Nikita Khrushchev, 1 December 1963

Chivalry in despair is the spirit of this letter written by Jackie Kennedy on one of her last nights in the White House, a week after the assassination of her husband John F. Kennedy. The President and his adversary the Soviet premier Nikita Khrushchev were opposites: Kennedy a handsome, cultured, millionaire Lothario, Khrushchev a warty, brutal Communist peasant. They had had bruising negotiations – and only narrowly avoided launching the world into nuclear war. There were many in the CIA who feared the Russians might have played a role in planning the assassination. Khrushchev, for his part, was terrified of being blamed for it. Perhaps the letter that follows is written to calm the Russian – it is certainly supremely elegant and touching in both its literary simplicity, presidential grandeur and its theory of Big Men and Little Men.

Dear Mr Chairman President,

I would like to thank you for sending Mr Mikoyan as your representative to my husband's funeral. He looked so upset when he came through the line, and I was very moved.

I tried to give him a message for you that day – but as it was such a terrible day for me, I do not know if my words came out as I meant them to.

So now, on one of the last nights I will spend in the White House, in one of the last letters I will write on this paper in the White House, I would like to write you my message.

I send it only because I know how much my husband cared about peace, and how the relation between you and him was central to this care in his mind. He used to quote your words in some of his speeches – 'in the next war the survivors will envy the dead'.

You and he were adversaries, but you were allied in a determination that the world should not be blown up. You respected each other and could deal with each other. I know that President Johnson will make every effort to establish the same relationship with you.

The danger which troubled my husband was that war might be started not so much by the big men as by the little ones.

While big men know the needs for self-control and restraint – little men are sometimes moved more by fear and pride. If only in the future the big men can continue to make the little ones sit down and talk, before they start to fight.

I know that President Johnson will continue the policy in which my husband so deeply believed – a policy of control and restraint – and he will need your help.

I send this letter because I know so deeply of the importance of the relationship which existed between you and my husband, and also because of your kindness, and that of Mrs. Khruschev in Vienna.

I read that she had tears in her eyes when she left the American Embassy in Moscow, after signing the book of mourning. Please thank her for that.

Sincerely,
Jacqueline Kennedy

Babur to his son Humayun, 11 January 1529

This is a letter of tolerance. Babur, born in 1483, was a prince descended from greatness, from the conqueror Tamurlane, in a family that had lost its glory. But almost single-handedly he restored its power, conquered the vastness of India and founded his own dynasty known as the Mughals. In the famous memoirs The Baburnama, Babur writes of battles and polo matches, feasts and poetry, but he also knew how to rule the complex multi-religious society of India. Here, aged forty-five, shortly before his death, Emperor Babur gives advice to his son that is relevant today not just in India but also in the wider Islamic world.

Oh my son! The realm of Hindustan is full of diverse creeds. Praise be to God, the Righteous, the Glorious, the Highest, that He hath granted unto thee the Empire of it. It is but proper that you, with heart cleansed of all religious

bigotry, should dispense justice according to the tenets of
each community. And in particular refrain from the sacrifice
of cow, for that way lies the conquest of the hearts of the
people of Hindustan; and the subjects of the realm will,
through royal favour, be devoted to thee. And the temples
and abodes of worship of every community under Imperial
sway, you should not damage. Dispense justice so that the
sovereign may be happy with the subjects and likewise the
subjects with their sovereign. The progress of Islam is better
by the sword of kindness, not by the sword of oppression.

Ignore the disputations of Shias and Sunnis; for therein is
the weakness of Islam. And bring together the subjects with
different beliefs in the manner of the Four Elements, so that
the body-politic may be immune from the various ailments.
And remember the deeds of Hazrat Taimur Sahib Qiran so
that you may become mature in matters of Government.
And on us is but the duty to advise.

Émile Zola to Félix Faure, 13 January 1898

This letter is a wonder of moral outrage. Zola's letter to the French
President exposes the injustice and anti-Semitism of the French military that has already divided France in a vicious schism between two
visions of the country: Catholic nationalism versus secular liberalism.
Zola exposes the 'shady creatures', shameful hypocrites and despicable
anti-Semites who have sentenced a totally innocent man to life on the
hellish Devil's Island prison in French Guiana for treason – even when,
two years later, they uncover the identity of the real German spy who
really is guilty of betraying his country.

In December 1894, a young French captain from Alsace named
Alfred Dreyfus, who happened to be Jewish, was convicted of selling
French military secrets to German intelligence. The conviction was
always highly suspect, but in 1896 French intelligence identified the real

culprit as Major Ferdinand Esterhazy. Nonetheless, the French generals and politicians arranged for Esterhazy to be acquitted and covered up his guilt. As the brazen injustice and rampant racism divide France, the novelist Émile Zola, author of *Nana* and *Germinal*, decides he must speak out, publishing this letter exposing the men behind the framing of Dreyfus, the public campaign of anti-Semitism, and the cover-up.

Zola was tried for libel and had to flee to London, but the letter worked: the outcry forced the government to reopen the case. In 1899, broken after five years in captivity, Dreyfus returned for a second trial. Amazingly he was convicted again and sentenced to ten years, but was then pardoned and exonerated, his rank reinstated, dying in 1935 as a lieutenant-colonel. In 1902 Zola died of carbon monoxide poisoning due to a blocked chimney: he may have been murdered for writing this letter. Its exposé of anti-semitism is sadly relevant today.

Mr President,

Would you allow me, grateful as I am for the kind reception you once extended to me, to show my concern about maintaining your well-deserved prestige and to point out that your star which, until now, has shone so brightly, risks being dimmed by the most shameful and indelible of stains?

Unscathed by vile slander, you have won the hearts of all. You are radiant in the patriotic glory of our country's alliance with Russia, you are about to preside over the solemn triumph of our World Fair, the jewel that crowns this great century of labour, truth, and freedom. But what filth this wretched Dreyfus affair has cast on your name – I wanted to say 'reign'. A court martial, under orders, has just dared to acquit a certain Esterhazy, a supreme insult to all truth and justice. And now the image of France is sullied by this filth, and history shall record that it was under your presidency that this crime against society was committed.

As they have dared, so shall I dare. Dare to tell the truth, as I have pledged to tell it, in full, since the normal channels of justice have failed to do so. My duty is to speak out; I do not wish to be an accomplice in this travesty. My nights would otherwise be haunted by the spectre of the innocent man, far away, suffering the most horrible of tortures for a crime he did not commit . . .

But now we see Dreyfus appearing before the court martial. Behind the closed doors, the utmost secrecy is demanded. Had a traitor opened the border to the enemy and driven the Kaiser straight to Notre-Dame the measures of secrecy and silence could not have been more stringent. The public was astounded; rumours flew of the most horrible acts, the most monstrous deceptions, lies that were an affront to our history. The public, naturally, was taken in. No punishment could be too harsh. The people clamoured for the traitor to be publicly stripped of his rank and demanded to see him writhing with remorse on his rock of infamy. Could these things be true, these unspeakable acts, these deeds so dangerous that they must be carefully hidden behind closed doors to keep Europe from going up in flames? No! They were nothing but the demented fabrications of Major du Paty de Clam, a cover-up of the most preposterous fantasies imaginable. To be convinced of this one need only read carefully the accusation as it was presented before the court martial.

How flimsy it is! The fact that someone could have been convicted on this charge is the ultimate iniquity. I defy decent men to read it without a stir of indignation in their hearts and a cry of revulsion, at the thought of the undeserved punishment being meted out there on Devil's Island. He knew several languages: a crime! He carried no compromising papers: a crime! He would occasionally visit his country of origin: a crime! He was hard-working, and strove to be well informed: a crime! He did not become

confused: a crime! He became confused: a crime! And how
childish the language is, how groundless the accusation! . . .

These, Sir, are the facts that explain how this miscarriage
of justice came about; The evidence of Dreyfus's character,
his affluence, the lack of motive and his continued
affirmation of innocence combine to show that he is the
victim of the lurid imagination of Major du Paty de Clam,
the religious circles surrounding him, and the 'dirty Jew'
obsession that is the scourge of our time.

And now we come to the Esterhazy case. Three years
have passed, many consciences remain profoundly troubled,
become anxious, investigate, and wind up convinced that
Dreyfus is innocent . . .

As I have shown, the Dreyfus case was a matter internal
to the War Office: an officer of the General Staff, denounced
by his co-officers of the General Staff, sentenced under
pressure by the Chiefs of Staff. Once again, he could not
be found innocent without the entire General Staff being
guilty. And so, by all means imaginable, by press campaigns,
by official communications, by influence, the War Office
covered up for Esterhazy only to condemn Dreyfus once
again . . . We are horrified by the terrible light the Dreyfus
affair has cast upon it all, this human sacrifice of an
unfortunate man, a 'dirty Jew'. Ah, what a cesspool of folly
and foolishness, what preposterous fantasies, what corrupt
police tactics, what inquisitorial, tyrannical practices! What
petty whims of a few higher-ups trampling the nation under
their boots, ramming back down their throats the people's
cries for truth and justice, with the travesty of state security
as a pretext . . .

It is a crime that those people who wish to see a generous
France take her place as leader of all the free and just
nations are being accused of fomenting turmoil in the
country, denounced by the very plotters who are conniving

so shamelessly to foist this miscarriage of justice on the entire world. It is a crime to lie to the public, to twist public opinion to insane lengths in the service of the vilest death-dealing machinations. It is a crime to poison the minds of the meek and the humble, to stoke the passions of reactionism and intolerance, by appealing to that odious anti-Semitism that, unchecked, will destroy the freedom-loving France of the Rights of Man. It is a crime to exploit patriotism in the service of hatred, and it is, finally, a crime to ensconce the sword as the modern god, whereas all science is toiling to achieve the coming era of truth and justice.

Truth and justice, so ardently longed for! How terrible it is to see them trampled, unrecognised and ignored! . . .

This is the plain truth, Mr. President, and it is terrifying. It will leave an indelible stain on your presidency. I realize that you have no power over this case, that you are limited by the Constitution and your entourage. You have, nonetheless, your duty as a man, which you will recognise and fulfil. As for myself, I have not despaired in the least, of the triumph of right. I repeat with the most vehement conviction: truth is on the march, and nothing will stop it . . .

I accuse Lt. Col. du Paty de Clam of being the diabolical creator of this miscarriage of justice . . . over the last three years, by all manner of ludicrous and evil machinations.

I accuse General Mercier of complicity, at least by mental weakness, in one of the greatest inequities of the century.

I accuse General Billot of having held in his hands absolute proof of Dreyfus's innocence and covering it up, and making himself guilty of this crime against mankind and justice, as a political expedient and a way for the compromised General Staff to save face . . .

I have but one passion: to enlighten those who have been kept in the dark, in the name of humanity which has suffered so much and is entitled to happiness. My fiery protest is simply the cry of my very soul. Let them dare, then, to bring me before a court of law and let the enquiry take place in broad daylight! I am waiting.

With my deepest respect, Sir.

Émile Zola, 13th January 1898

Lorenzo the Magnificent to Giovanni de Medici, 23 March 1492

Every boy of sixteen should receive a letter like this from his father telling him to stay clear of debauchery and concentrate on his work. This one is special because the son Giovanni has just become the youngest ever cardinal in the history of the Catholic Church. He already has a proven tendency to over-indulge his sensual appetites in terms of both food and women. And his father is Lorenzo the Magnificent, the head of the house of Medici, a vastly wealthy banker, ruthless political player and brilliant patron of Renaissance art who has effectively ruled the republican city-state of Florence since 1469. Now Lorenzo is older and in decline but he has just managed to achieve his ambition to arrange the elevation of his son Giovanni to the scarlet of cardinal which means the Medici are diversifying their power into the Church and into Rome. So the boy is setting off for Rome, a city rightly called a 'sink of iniquity' where there are said to be 7,000 prostitutes in a population of just 50,000. Lorenzo is a tender father as you can see in his wonderful letter full of sensible advice like 'Eat plain food and take plenty of exercise' and 'oppose temptation'. But Rome is about to become even more lascivious: the Borgias are coming to power . . .

Just after Giovanni's departure for Rome, his magnificent father died and the Medicis temporarily lost control of Florence. Cheerful, hedonistic and fat, Cardinal de Medici enjoyed his career in Rome, finally in 1513 contriving to be elected Pope as Leo X, the very definition of the decadent, venal pontiff who inspired Martin Luther's revolt against the corrupt Church. On his election, he is said to have announced:

'Since God has given us the papacy, let us enjoy it.' He died in 1521 after thoroughly enjoying every minute.

The first thing I want to impress upon you is that you ought to be grateful to God, remembering always that it is not through *your* merits, or *your* wisdom that you have gained this dignity, but through *His* favour. Show your thankfulness by a holy, exemplary, chaste life . . . During the past year I have been much comforted to see that, without being told, to do so, you have often of your own accord gone to confession and to Holy Communion. I do not think there is a better way of keeping in God's grace than to make this a regular practice. I know only too well that in going to live in Rome, which is a sink of iniquity, you will find it hard to follow this advice because there will be many there who will try to corrupt you and incite you to vice, and because your promotion to the cardinalate at your early age arouses much envy . . . You must, therefore, opposite temptation all the more firmly . . . It is at the same time necessary that you should not incur a reputation for hypocrisy, and in conversation not to affect either austerity or undue seriousness. You will understand all this better when you are older . . . You are well aware how important is the example you ought to show to others as a cardinal, and that the world would be a better place if all cardinals were what they ought to be, because if they ever were so there would always be a good Pope and consequently a more peaceful world . . .

You are the youngest cardinal, not only in the Sacred College of today but at any time in the past. Therefore, when you are in assembly with other cardinals, you must be the most unassuming, and the most humble . . . Try to live with regularity . . . Silk and jewels are seldom suitable to those in your station. Much better to collect antiquities and beautiful books, and to maintain a learned and well regulated household rather than a grand one. Invite others to your house more often than you accept invitations to theirs; but not too often. Eat plain food and take plenty of exercise . . . confide in others too little rather than too much. One rule above all others I urge you to observe most rigorously: *Rise early in the morning.* This is not only for your health's sake, but also so that you cab arrange and expedite all the day's business . . .

With regard to your speaking in the Consistory, I think it would be best for the present while you are still so young, to refer whatever is proposed to you to His Holiness, giving as your reason your youth and inexperience. You will find that you will be asked to intercede with the Pope for many small objects. Try at first to do this as seldom as you can, and not to worry him unduly in this way. For it is the Pope's nature to pay the most attention to those who bother him least . . .

Farewell.

Liberation

Emmeline Pankhurst to the Women's Social and Political Union, 10 January 1913

Emmeline Pankhurst demands a militant campaign to acquire votes for women, including smashing windows and arson. Pankhurst's methods appalled many, including her daughters Adela and Sylvia, who left the Women's Social and Political Union (WSPU) in protest; many other prominent activists claimed that the extremists of the WSPU 'were the chief obstacles in the way of the success of the suffrage movement in the House of Commons'. Nonetheless, Pankhurst's methods worked. She placed female suffrage at the centre of the national agenda.

Born in Manchester, married to a much elder barrister, a supporter of the female suffrage movement, with whom she had five children, Pankhurst was a highly effective campaigner. She, her daughters and her supporters known as the Suffragettes organised violent protests and assaults on policemen, were imprisoned, went on hunger strike, were force-fed and beaten several times. Only the First World War stopped her protests, but ironically it was the war that made female suffrage undeniable. In 1918 votes were granted to women who were householders over the age of thirty. This was extended to women over twenty-one in 1928 – just before Pankhurst's death.

> LINCOLN'S INN HOUSE, KINGSWAY, W.C.
> Private and Confidential

Dear Friend,

The Prime Minister has announced that in the week beginning January 20th, the Women's Amendments to the Manhood Suffrage Bill will be discussed and voted upon. This means that within a few short days the fate of these Amendments will be finally decided.

The W.S.P.U. has from the first declined to call any truce on the strength of the Prime Minister's so-called pledge, and has refused to depend upon the Amendments in question, because the Government have not accepted the responsibility of getting them carried. There are, however, some Suffragists – and there may be some even in the ranks of the W.S.P.U. – who hope against hope that in spite of the Government's intrigues an unofficial Amendment may be carried. Feeling as they do, these Suffragists are tempted to hold their hand as far as militancy is concerned, until after the fate of the Amendments is known.

But every member of the W.S.P.U. recognises that the defeat of the Amendments will make militancy more a moral duty and more a political necessity than it has ever been before. We must prepare beforehand to deal with that situation!

There are degrees of militancy. Some women are able to go further than others in militant action and each woman is the judge of her own duty so far as that is concerned. To be militant in some way or other is, however, a moral obligation. It is a duty which every woman will owe to her own conscience and self-respect, to other women who are less fortunate than she herself is, and to all those who are to come after her.

If any woman refrains from militant protest against the injury done by the Government and the House of Commons to women and to the race, she will share the responsibility for the crime. Submission under such circumstances will be itself a crime.

I know that the defeat of the Amendments will prove to thousands of women that to rely only on peaceful, patient methods, is to court failure, and that militancy is inevitable.

We must, as I have said, prepare to meet the crisis before it arises. Will you therefore tell me (by letter, if it is not possible to do so by word of mouth), that you are ready to take your share in manifesting in a practical manner your indignation at the betrayal of our cause.

Yours sincerely, E. Pankhurst

Rosa Parks to Jessica Mitford, 26 February 1956

The mother of the civil rights movement in America, Rosa Parks, then around forty-three, was already an activist along with her husband when she took on the racist law in Montgomery, Alabama, that ordered the segregation of white and black people on the local buses. This was just one of the notorious 'Jim Crow' laws brought in throughout the Southern states in the early twentieth century, enforcing repression of black people even though slavery had been abolished forty years earlier. Parks had helped investigate some of the racist atrocities – gang rapes and murders of people of colour – that so often went unpunished in Alabama.

In December 1955 Parks refused to give up her seat in the 'coloured' section of the bus she was travelling in to a white passenger when the 'white' section was full. She was arrested, and her case was used in the subsequent legal challenge against segregation that was won in November 1956. In the middle of the case, before its outcome is known, Parks writes this letter to 'Mrs Treuhaft,' who is better known as Jessica Mitford, the most radical of the six daughters of the English nobleman Lord Redesdale. One became a duchess, two were Nazi sympathisers, one was a novelist and Jessica became a Communist. At this time she is married to Robert Treuhaft, a civil rights lawyer living in California. This story is not over. This letter marks just one stage in the long history of the struggle against racism in America, starting with the American Civil War, continuing with the work of Martin Luther King in the 1960s – and essential today with movements like Black Lives Matter.

Dear Mrs. Treuhaft:

I am very happy to hear from you again. Thanks,

very much for the contribution and the names of other contributors.

We are having a difficult time here, but we are not discouraged. The increased pressure seems to strengthen us for the next blow.

My first case was heard in the Circuit Court February 22, I was found guilty and sentenced to 70 days in jail. The appeal was made to the State Supreme Court.

I was immediately arrested again with the leaders of the bus protest.

We have received very generous contributions from over the country, although no specific appeal has been made through the mail.

The wide spread publicity we are getting is most disturbing to the local governing group. They resent outside interference. Therefore, I will have to take the matter of direct appeal to the Montgomery Improvement Association.

The Claudette Colvin Case is one of four filed with the Federal Court at present.

I will write again soon.

Sincerely yours,

Rosa L. Parks

Nelson Mandela to Winnie Mandela, 2 April 1969

Mandela's prison letters to Winnie are lessons on how to live. Born into Tembu royalty in 1918, Mandela joined the African National Congress and the armed struggle against apartheid as a lawyer in Johannesburg in the 1950s. Seven years later Nelson spotted a young woman, Winnie Madikizela, aged twenty-two, at a bus stop. Divorcing his wife, he married Winnie. At the Rivonia Trial in 1964 Mandela was sentenced to life imprisonment for terrorism.

Mandela's inspirational prison letters show his gift for self improvement, his astonishing humility and natural decency. During twenty-seven years in prison, as he explains to Winnie here, Mandela regards his cell as 'an ideal place to learn to know yourself, to search realistically and regularly the process of your own mind and feelings. In judging our progress as individuals we tend to concentrate on external factors such as one's social position, influence and popularity, wealth and standard of education. These are, of course, important . . . and it is perfectly understandable if many people exert themselves mainly to achieve all these. But internal factors may be even more crucial in assessing one's development as a human being. Honesty, sincerity, simplicity, humility, pure generosity, absence of vanity, readiness to serve others – qualities which are within easy reach of every soul – are the foundation of one's spiritual life. Development in matters of this nature is inconceivable without serious introspection, without knowing yourself, your weaknesses and mistakes. At least, if for nothing else, the cell gives you the opportunity to look daily into your entire conduct, to overcome the bad and develop whatever is good in you. Regular meditation, say about 15 minutes a day before you turn in, can be very fruitful in this regard. You may find it difficult at first to pinpoint the negative features in your life, but the 10th attempt may yield rich rewards. Never forget that a saint is a sinner who keeps on trying.'

During his long ordeal, Winnie struggled without his guidance, enforcing her power in Soweto through a security unit of murderous thugs called the Mandela United Football Team. Released in 1990 and then elected president, Mandela oversaw the transfer of power from white rule to multiracial democracy without bloodshed – one of the towering achievements of the twentieth century.

Mandela divorced Winnie in 1992 and married Graça, the widow of President Machel of Mozambique. Mandela died in 2013, Winnie five years later. This letter, signed 'Dalibunga', his Xhosa tribal name, is one of his best.

Darling,

I was taken completely by surprise to learn that you had been very unwell as I did not have even the slightest hint that you suffered from blackouts. I have known of your heart condition & pleurisy attacks.

The Power of Positive Thinking & The Results of Positive Thinking, both written by the American psychologist Dr Norman Vincent Peale, may be rewarding to read.

He makes the basic point that it is not so much the disability one suffers from that matters but one's attitude to it. The man who says: I will conquer this illness & live a happy life, is already halfway to victory.

Of the talents you possess, the one that attracts me most is your courage & determination. This makes you stand head & shoulders above the average & will in the end bring you the triumph of high achievement. Do consciously keep this constantly in mind.

You look somewhat sad, absent-minded & unwell but lovely all the same [in a family photo]. The [photo] depicts all I know in you, the devastating beauty & charm which ten stormy years of married life have not chilled. I suspect that you intended the picture to convey a special message that no words could ever express. Rest assured I have caught it. All that I wish to say now is that the picture has aroused all the tender feelings in me & softened the grimness that is all around. It has sharpened my longing for you & our sweet & peaceful home.

Finally Mhlope, I should like you to know that if in the past my letters have not been passionate, it is because I need not seek to improve the debt I owe to a woman who, in spite of formidable difficulties & lack of experience, has nonetheless succeeded in keeping the home fires burning & in attending to the smallest wants & wishes of her incarcerated life companion. These things make me humble

to be the object of your love & affection. Remember that
hope is a powerful weapon even when all else is lost. You
are in my thoughts every moment of my life. Nothing will
happen to you darling. You will certainly recover and rise.

A million kisses & tons & tons of love.

Dalibunga

Abram Hannibal to Peter the Great, 5 March 1722

The first black general and engineer of modern times was a Russian
African named Abram Hannibal. He was captured by slave traders as
a boy, probably in West Africa; sold in Istanbul, and there bought by
agents of Tsar Peter the Great, who brought him to Russia where 'I
was baptised by the Tsar-Emperor and His Majesty chose to stand as
my godfather'. Henceforth he was known as Abram Petrovich ('Son of
Peter') Hannibal because many black men were called 'Hannibal' after
the Carthaginian general (though in fact he was Phoenician). Hannibal
often served as Peter's equerry; the tsar recognised the boy's talent,
sending him to be trained in engineering, artillery and mathematics
in Paris, where he ran out of money. Here Hannibal appeals to Peter,
who bails him out, ordering his chancellor: 'Abram the Moor has written from Paris that he is ready to come back to Russia only he has
to settle debts of 200 gold écu ... Please send money and travel expenses and tell Abram to leave for Petersburg.' By Catherine the Great's
reign, Hannibal was a general; he was the great-grandfather of the
poet Pushkin.

Do you remember Your Majesty how you warned me five
years ago not to fall into bad habits or end up in prison.
Instead you told me if I worked hard at my studies for the
glory of Russia you would never desert me. Well I didn't let
you down but we are all of us in debt here not because of
delinquency on our party but simply we are victims of paper

money with terrible consequences as I am sure Count Musin Pushkin told you were it not for his kindness I would have surely died of hunger.

Between Simón Bolívar, Manuela Sáenz and James Thorne, 1822–23

Here are two goodbye letters in the love triangle of the Liberator of South America. 'I am the genius of the storm,' declared Simón Bolívar, known as El Libertador, who in a just a few frantic years of fighting the Spanish, freed the modern states of Colombia, Venezuela, Panama, Ecuador, Peru and Bolivia – half of a vast continent. Only Napoleon Bonaparte had achieved anything resembling the conquests of Bolívar. But he was also an enthusiastic dancer and lover, often greeted by devoted young girls as he liberated their cities, claiming that sex and flirtation stimulated his genius: 'I deliberated best when I was at the centre of revelry amongst the pleasures of a ball.' And the genius of the storm met his match in Manuela Sáenz.

After becoming President of Gran Colombia in 1819, Bolívar marched across the Andes to conquer Ecuador where he met twenty-two-year-old Manuela, the illegitimate daughter of a Spanish nobleman and mixed-race mother, a convent girl who had been seduced by an officer, then married off to James Thorne, an older English merchant. Flamboyant, fearless, intelligent and sensuous, she became Bolívar's supporter and lover. But Bolívar fears any commitment, sounding much like anyone feeling suffocated in a relationship: 'give me time'. He tries to restrain Manuela's enthusiasm, and sends her back to her husband.

Simón Bolívar to Manuela Sáenz, 3 July 1822

I want to answer, most beautiful Manuela, your demands of love, which are entirely reasonable. But I have to be candid with you, who have given me so much of yourself . . . it's

time you knew that long ago I loved a woman as only the
young can love. Out of respect, I never talk about it. I'm
pondering these things, and I want to give you time to do
the same, because your words lure me; because I know that
this may well be my moment to love you and for us to love
one another. I need time to get used to this, for a military
life is neither easy to endure nor easy to leave behind. I have
fooled death so many times now that death dogs my every
step . . . Allow me to be sure of myself – of you . . . I cannot
lie. I never lie! My passion for you is wild, and you know it.
Give me time.

And here is Manuela's response: she writes this amazing letter to her
husband, copying it to Bolívar to make sure there is no way back to her
tedious marriage: her destiny is with Bolívar, whom she then follows
to Bogotá.

Manuela Sáenz to James Thorne, 1823

No, no, no, hombre! A thousand times No! Sir, you are an
excellent person, indeed one of a kind – that I will never
deny. I only regret that you are not a better man so that
my leaving you would honour Bolívar more. I know very
well that I can never be joined to him in what you call
honour. Do you think I am any less honourable because
he is my lover, not my husband? Ah! I do not live by social
conventions men construct to torment us. So leave me be,
my dear Englishman. We will marry again in heaven but not
on this earth . . . On earth, you are a boring man. Up there in
the celestial heights, everything will be so English, because
a life of monotony was invented for you people, who make
love without pleasure, conversation without grace – who
walk slowly, greet solemnly, move heavily, joke without
laughing . . . But enough of my cheekiness. With all the

sobriety, truth, and clarity of an Englishwoman, I say now: I will never return for you. You are a protestant and I a pagan – that should be obstacle enough. But I am also in love with another man, and that is the greater, stronger reason. You see how precise my mind can be?

Your invariable friend, Manuela

Manuela fought beside Bolívar, helped with his papers, nursed the wounded and deserved her promotion to colonel. There was something utterly liberated about Manuela: she sported dashing male uniforms, had affairs with black servants and female lovers, defied all convention.

In Bogotá's presidential palace in 1828, assassins forced their way into Bolívar's bedroom. Manuela fought them off and was almost beaten to death, enabling The Liberator to escape. Henceforth he called her 'Libertadora de Libertador' – the liberatrix of the liberator. Bolívar retired from power and died of tuberculosis, aged forty-seven, in 1830. Manuela, persecuted, died in penury in 1856. In 2007, she was posthumously promoted to a general of Ecuador and in 2010 given a state funeral in Venezuela.

Fate

Oscar Wilde to Robert Ross, 28 February 1895

Even though he didn't yet know it, this letter marks the beginning of the ruin of Oscar Wilde. The author of *The Importance of Being Earnest*, *The Picture of Dorian Gray*, and stories for children and adults such as 'The Happy Prince', Wilde was celebrated for his wit and his success. When he arrived in America, he told the customs officials 'I have nothing to declare but my genius', then made a fortune on a sell-out lecture tour. Son of a Dublin surgeon, Wilde was married with children but he was also ostentatiously gay at a time when homosexuality was illegal. He loved the adventure of pursuing wild encounters, which he called 'feasting with panthers', but he was in love with a spoilt aristocrat named Lord Alfred 'Bosie' Douglas, whose monstrous father the Marquess of Queensberry was a pugilistic and bigoted ruffian. On this day, Queensberry left a provocative and misspelt card at Wilde's club, calling him a 'Somdomite'. In this letter, Wilde reports Queensberry's insult to his best friend, literary executor and sometime lover Robbie Ross, who like everyone else begs him not to take the bait. But Wilde insists on suing Queensberry for libel, a folly that would lead inexorably to his exposure as a homosexual, his trial and sentencing to prison with hard labour: it destroyed him.

Hotel Avondale, Piccadilly

Dearest Bobbie,

Since I saw you something has happened. Bosie's father has left a card at my club with hideous words on it. I don't see anything but a criminal prosecution.

My whole life seems ruined by this man. The tower of ivory is assailed by the foul thing. On the sand is my life spilt. I don't know what to do. If you could come here at 11.30 please do so tonight. I mar your life by trespassing ever on your love and kindness. I have asked Bosie to come tomorrow.

Ever yours

Oscar

Between Alexander Hamilton and Aaron Burr, June 1804

The letters that follow chart the destruction of the most brilliant mind of the American Founding Fathers by the most despicable. The musical *Hamilton* has retold the story using hip-hop music, but here are the real letters. Alexander Hamilton was the illegitimate prodigy born on a Caribbean island who made it to America, became aide to George Washington, designer of the American Constitution and the first Treasury Secretary as well as an army general. He possessed all the turbulence of genius but also, in an era obsessed with a complex code of honour, the touchiness of the self-invented.

Aaron Burr, also a veteran of the War of Independence, had all Hamilton's ambition but lacked his brilliance, and he seethed with jealousy particularly when Hamilton helped undermine his career by backing his old enemy Thomas Jefferson against him, Burr, his supposed friend, in the presidential elections of 1800. Burr was instead elected Vice President under Jefferson, but the President despised and excluded him. Hamilton himself was out of power after the collapse of his Federalist Party. Using the orotund language of honour and law (both being lawyers), Burr accuses Hamilton of defaming him in the 1804 contest for the governorship of New York. Under the exaggeratedly polite phrases the reader can feel the oncoming resort to violence – in the form of a duel – and then we read the arrangements being made by their seconds, William P. Van Ness and Nathaniel Pendleton.

The duel is fought on 11 July 1804, in New Jersey. Hamilton claimed he would fire in the air. Burr shoots at Hamilton, killing him. Burr was charged with his murder, but was never tried. He lived on until 1836, perhaps the most despised man in early American history.

Burr to Hamilton

N York 18 June 1804

Sir,

I send for your perusal a letter signed Ch. D. Cooper
which, though apparently published some time ago, has
but very recently come to my knowledge. Mr. Van Ness,
who does me the favor to deliver this, will point out to you
that clause of the letter to which I particularly request your
attention.

You must perceive, Sir, the necessity of a prompt and
unqualified acknowledgment or denial of the use of any
expressions which could warrant the assertions of Dr.
Cooper.

I have the honor to be
Your Obdt. St
A. Burr

Hamilton to Burr

N York 20 June 1804

Sir:

I have maturely reflected on the subject of your letter of
the 18th Instant, and the more I have reflected, the more I
have become convinced that I could not without manifest
impropriety make the avowal or disavowal which you seem
to think necessary. The clause pointed out by Mr. Van Ness
is in these terms: 'I could detail to you a still more despicable
opinion which General Hamilton has expressed of Mr. Burr.'
To endeavor to discover the meaning of this declaration, I
was obliged to seek in the antecedent part of the letter for
the opinion to which it referred, as having been already
disclosed. I found it in these words: 'Genl. Hamilton and

Judge Kent have declared in substance that they looked upon
Mr. Burr to be a dangerous man, and one who ought not to
be trusted with the reins of Government.' The language of
Dr. Cooper plainly implies that he considered this opinion
of you, which he attributes to me, as a despicable one;
but he affirms that I have expressed some other still more
despicable; without, however, mentioning to whom, when
or where. 'Tis evident that the phrase 'still more despicable'
admits of infinite shades from very light to very dark. How
am I to judge of the degree intended. Or how should I annex
any precise idea to language so vague?

Between Gentlemen despicable and still more despicable
are not worth the pains of a distinction. When, therefore,
you do not interrogate me as to the opinion which is
specifically ascribed to me, I must conclude that you view it
as within the limits to which the animadversions of political
opponents, upon each other, may justifiably extend; and
consequently as not warranting the idea of it which Dr.
Cooper appears to entertain. If so, what precise inference
could you draw as a guide for your future conduct, were I
to acknowledge that I had expressed an opinion of you, still
more despicable than the one which is particularized? How
could you be sure that even this opinion had exceeded the
bounds which you would yourself deem admissible between
political opponents?

But I forbear further comment on the embarrassment to
which the requisition you have made naturally leads. The
occasion forbids a more ample illustration, though nothing
would be more easy than to pursue it.

Repeating that I can not reconcile it with propriety to
make the acknowledgment or denial you desire, I will
add that I deem it inadmissible on principle, to consent to
be interrogated as to the justness of the inferences which
may be drawn by others, from whatever I may have said

of a political opponent in the course of a fifteen years competition. If there were no other objection to it, this is sufficient, that it would tend to expose my sincerity and delicacy to injurious imputations from every person who may at any time have conceived that import of my expressions differently from what I may then have intended, or may afterwards recollect.

I stand ready to avow or disavow promptly and explicitly any precise or definite opinion which I may be charged with having declared to any gentleman. More than this can not fitly be expected from me; and especially it can not reasonably be expected that I shall enter into an explanation upon a basis so vague as that which you have adopted. I trust upon more reflection you will see the matter in the same light with me. If not, I can only regret the circumstances and must abide the consequences.

The publication of Dr. Cooper was never seen by me 'till after the receipt of your letter.

Sir, I have the honor to be

Your Obdt. St

A. Hamilton

Burr to Hamilton

N York 21 June, 1804

Sir,

Your letter of the 20th inst. has been this day received. Having considered it attentively, I regret to find in it nothing of that sincerity and delicacy which you profess to value.

Political opposition can never absolve gentlemen from the necessity of a rigid adherence to the laws of honor and the rules of decorum. I neither claim such privilege nor indulge it in others.

The common sense of mankind affixes to the epithet adopted by Dr. Cooper the idea of dishonor. It has been publicly applied to me under the sanction of your name. The question is not whether he has understood the meaning of the word or has used it according to syntax and with grammatical accuracy, but whether you have authorized this application either directly or by uttering expression or opinion derogatory to my honor. The time 'when' is in your own knowledge but no way material to me, as the calumny has now just been disclosed so as to become the subject of my notice and as the effect is present and palpable.

Your letter has furnished me with new reasons for requiring a definite reply.

I have the honor to be
Your Obdt. St
A. Burr

Hamilton to Burr

N York 22 June 1804

Sir,

Your first letter, in a style too peremptory, made a demand, in my opinion, unprecedented and unwarrantable. My answer, pointing out the embarrassment, gave you an opportunity to take a less exceptionable course. You have not chosen to do it, but by your last letter, received this day, containing expressions indecorous and improper, you have increased the difficulties to explanation, intrinsically incident to the nature of your application.

If by a 'definite reply' you mean the direct avowal or disavowal required in your first letter, I have no other answer to give than that which has already been given. If you mean anything different admitting of greater latitude, it is requisite you should explain.

I have the honor to be, Sir

Your Obdt. St

A. Hamilton

Van Ness to Pendleton, 26 June 1804

Sir,

The letter which you yesterday delivered me and your subsequent communication in Col. Burr's opinion evince no disposition on the part of Genl. Hamilton to come to a satisfactory accommodation. The injury complained of and the reparation expected are so definitely expressed in his (Col. B.'s) letter of the 21st Inst. that there is not perceived a necessity for further explanation on his part. The difficulty that would result from confining the inquiry to any particular times and occasions must be manifest. The denial of a specified conversation only, would leave strong implications that on other occasions improper language had been used. When and where injurious expressions and opinions have been uttered by Genl. Hamilton must be best known to him and of him only does Col. Burr think it proper to enquire.

No denial or declaration will be satisfactory unless it be general so as to wholly exclude the idea that rumors derogatory to Col. Burr's honor can have originated with Genl. Hamilton or have been fairly inferred from anything he has said. A definite reply to a requisition of this nature is demanded in Col. Burr's letter of the 21st Inst. This being refused, invites the alternative alluded to in Genl. H.'s letter of the 20th Inst. It was demanded by the position in which the controversy was placed by Genl. H. on the 22nd Inst., and I was immediately furnished with a communication demanding a personal interview.

The necessity of this measure has not in the opinion of Col. Burr been diminished by the General's last letter or any subsequent communication which has been received and I am again instructed to deliver you a message as soon as it may be convenient for you to receive it. I beg, therefore, you will have the politeness to inform me at what hour I shall wait on you.

Your most obt. & very hum. Servt.

W. P. Van Ness

Anonymous to Lord Monteagle, October 1605

The plan was to change the course of English history in the most nihilistic and diabolical way imaginable. After struggling for years during the long Protestant reign of Elizabeth I, a terrorist cell of Anglo-Catholics led by Robert Catesby lost patience with the new king James I and conspired to plant gunpowder beneath the Houses of Parliament so as to murder the entire elite of the kingdom: king, queen, princes, lords and gentlemen, a crime that would have been considerably more horrific and effective than 9/11. The cell was small enough to succeed and might easily have done so, had not one of its members delivered a warning letter, anonymously, to Lord Monteagle. Having recently nearly lost his head as a participant in Lord Essex's rebellion against Queen Elizabeth, Monteagle rushes the letter to the chief minister Robert Cecil, earl of Salisbury, who shows it to the king. Cecil allows the pompous monarch the credit for interpreting the key words 'terrible blow' and for ordering a search that reveals the cellar filled with gunpowder, guarded by the conspirator and explosives expert Guy Fawkes. The plot is foiled, the terrorists executed and their failure still celebrated every year with bonfires on 5 November: Guy Fawkes Day.

My Lord, out of the love I bear to some of your friends, I have a care of your preservation. Therefore I would advise you, as you tender your life, to devise some excuse to shift your attendance at this Parliament; for God and man hath concurred to punish the wickedness of this time. And think not slightly of this advertisement, but retire yourself into your country where you may expect the event in safety. For though there be no appearance of any stir, yet I say they shall receive a terrible blow this Parliament; and yet they shall not see who hurts them. This counsel is not to be condemned because it may do you good and can do you no harm; for the danger is passed as soon as you have burnt the letter. And I hope God will give you the grace to make good use of it, to whose holy protection I commend you.

Babur to Humayun, 25 December 1526

The targets of assassination attempts often die; sometimes they survive – but they rarely write a detailed letter about the experience and their vengeance. But then there are very few characters as extraordinary as Babur, the first emperor of Mughal India, conqueror, poet, memoirist, lover. In 1526 he invades India. He captures Delhi and kills the ruling sultan of the Lodi dynasty, Ibrahim, in battle. But he spares Ibrahim's mother Buwa and allows her to live on in the palace. Typically Babur decides to try Indian food and keeps four Indian chefs to do so. When Buwa hears this, she persuades the imperial chefs to poison the new emperor. Somehow Babur survives. His enemies had plotted his downfall. Instead it heralds their own: as he explains, he devises terrible deaths for the four assassins. The whole episode is recounted in a unique letter to his son Humayun, who then rules his Afghan territories from Kabul, in Babur's own flamboyant and vivid style.

On Friday the sixteenth of Rabi' [21 December] a strange incident took place . . . The wretched Buwa, mother of Ibrahim, heard that I was eating foods prepared by Hindustani cooks. This came about because three or four months prior to this date, since I had never seen Hindustani food, I said that Ibrahim's cooks should be brought. Of fifty or sixty cooks I kept four. So, having heard of this, she sent a man to Etawah to obtain a tola of poison wrapped up in a piece of paper and then give it to an old woman servant, who would then pass it to Ahmad Chashnigir. (In Hindustan they call the taster *chashnigir*, and a tola is a measure slightly more than two mithcals, as has been described.) ahmad gave it to the Hindustani cook in our kitchen, promising him four parganas to introduce it somehow to my food. After the first old woman, who gave Ahmad Chashnigir the poison, she sent another to see whether or not he had given me the poison. it is good that he put it on the plate and not in the pot, having done so because I had given the cooks strict instructions to supervise the Hindustanis and make them taste from the pot while our food was being prepared. When the meal was being dished out, however, our wretched cooks were negligent. The cook put a piece of thin bread on the porcelain plate and then sprinkled less than half of the poison from the paper on top of the bread. On top of the poison he put some meat dressed in oil. If he had sprinkled the poison on the meat, or if he had thrown it into the pot, it would have been bad. In a fluster, he threw the rest into the stove.

Late Friday evening they served the food. I ate a lot of rabbit stew and had quite a bit of dressed saffroned meat. I also had one or two titbits from the top of the poisoned Hindustani food. I took the dressed meat and ate it. There was no apparent bad taste. I had one or two pieces of dried meat. I felt sick. The day before, when I was eating dried meat, there had been an off-taste, so I thought that was the reason. Once again my stomach churned. While seated at the meal I felt sick two or three times and almost threw up. Finally I said to myself, 'Enough of this.' I got up and on my way to the toilet I almost threw up once. When I got to the toilet I vomited a lot. I never vomited after meals, not even when drinking. A cloud of suspicion came over my mind. I ordered the cook to be held while the vomit was given to a dog that was watched. Until near the end of the first watch the next morning the dog was pretty listless and its stomach was swollen. No matter how many stones they threw at it to try and get it to move, it refused to get up. It remained like that until midday, but then it got up and did not die. One or two pages had eaten the same food, and the next morning they too threw up a lot. One was very ill, but in the end they all recovered completely. 'Calamity struck, but all's well that ends well.' God gave me life anew; I had returned from the brink of death; I was born again. 'Wounded, I died and came to life again, Now I have learned the value of life.' I ordered Sultan-Muhammad Bakhshï to keep a close watch on the cook. When he was tortured he confessed the details given above.

On Monday I ordered the nobles, grandees, amirs, and ministers to attend court. The two men and two women were brought in for questioning. They confessed to all the details of the affair. I ordered the taster to be hacked to pieces and the cook to be skinned alive. One of the two women I had thrown under the elephants' feet, and the other I had shot. I had Buwa put under arrest. She will pay for what she has done.

On Saturday I drank a cup of milk. On Sunday I drank a cup of milk. I also drank some earth of Lemnos and opiate in milk and drank it. The milk really shook up my insides. On Saturday, the first day of this medication, I excreted some pitch-black things like burnt bile. Thank goodness now everything is all right. I never knew how precious life was. There is a line of poetry that says, 'He who reaches the point of death appreciates life.' Every time I think of this dreadful incident I get angry. It was by God's grace that I was given a new lease on life. How can I express my thanks?

Hoping this will not occasion alarm, I have described in detail everything that happened. Although it was a dreadful incident that cannot be adequately described by words, thank God I have lived to see another day, and all's well that ends well. Do not worry.

Nikita Khrushchev to John F. Kennedy, 24–26 October 1962

Two letters: one almost brings the world to the brink of nuclear annihilation and one brings it back. When US spy planes spot Soviet nuclear missiles on the Communist-ruled island of Cuba, President Kennedy faces probably the greatest crisis confronted by any commander-in-chief. America cannot allow the missiles to remain there and threaten American cities, yet any attempt to remove them may spark apocalyptic war. The young president imposes a blockade on the island, turning back further Soviet ships. The Soviet leader, Nikita Khrushchev, writes an aggressive letter that threatens war. The crisis darkens. Two days later, a second, more conciliatory letter arrives. Kennedy agonizes over their meaning. Finally, Kennedy decides to ignore the aggressive letter and simply answer the conciliatory one. A deal is agreed – Khrushchev to withdraw his missiles, Kennedy never to invade Cuba – and secretly to remove US missiles from Turkey. If for nothing else, Kennedy's conduct justifies his reputation. As for Cuba, its Marxist leader Fidel Castro had been willing to risk nuclear catastrophe and never forgave Khrushchev's betrayal. As for Khrushchev, his comrades were infuriated by his erratic recklessness and overthrew him a few months later.

Moscow, October 24, 1962

Dear Mr. President: I have received your letter of October
23, I have studied it, and am answering you.

Just imagine, Mr. President, that we had presented
you with the conditions of an ultimatum which you have
presented us by your action. How would you have reacted
to this? I think that you would have been indignant at such a
step on our part. And this would have been understandable
to us. In presenting us with these conditions, you, Mr.
President, have flung a challenge at us. Who asked you to do
this? By what right did you do this? . . . You, Mr. President,
are not declaring a quarantine, but rather are setting forth an
ultimatum and threatening that if we do not give in to your
demands you will use force. Consider what you are saying!
And you want to persuade me to agree to this! . . . No, Mr.
President, I cannot agree to this, and I think that in your
own heart you recognize that I am correct. I am convinced
that in my place you would act the same way. . .And we
also say—no . . . The Soviet Government considers that the
violation of the freedom to use international waters and
international air space is an act of aggression which pushes
mankind toward the abyss of a world nuclear-missile war.
Therefore, the Soviet Government cannot instruct the
captains of Soviet vessels bound for Cuba to observe the
orders of American naval forces blockading that Island. Our
instructions to Soviet mariners are to observe strictly the
universally accepted norms of navigation in international
waters and not to retreat one step from them. And if the
American side violates these rules, it must realize what
responsibility will rest upon it in that case. Naturally we
will not simply be bystanders with regard to piratical acts
by American ships on the high seas. We will then be forced

on our part to take the measures we consider necessary and adequate in order to protect our rights. We have everything necessary to do so.

Respectfully,

N. Khrushchev

Moscow, October 26, 1962, 7 p.m.

Dear Mr. President: I have received your letter of October 25. From your letter, I got the feeling that you have some understanding of the situation which has developed and (some) sense of responsibility. I value this . . . I think you will understand me correctly if you are really concerned about the welfare of the world. Everyone needs peace . . . War is our enemy and a calamity for all the peoples . . . I see, Mr. President, that you too are not devoid of a sense of anxiety for the fate of the world understanding, and of what war entails. What would a war give you? You are threatening us with war . . . In the name of the Soviet Government and the Soviet people, I assure you that your conclusions regarding offensive weapons on Cuba are groundless . . . You are mistaken if you think that any of our means on Cuba are offensive. However, let us not quarrel now. It is apparent that I will not be able to convince you of this . . . But, Mr. President, do you really seriously think that Cuba can attack the United States and that even we together with Cuba can attack you from the territory of Cuba? Can you really think that way? How is it possible? We do not understand this . . . If you are really concerned about the peace and welfare of your people, and this is your responsibility as President, then I, as the Chairman of the Council of Ministers, am concerned for my people. Moreover, the preservation of world peace should be our joint concern, since if, under contemporary conditions, war should break out, it would be a war not only between the reciprocal claims, but a worldwide cruel and destructive war . . . If assurances were given by the President and the Government of the United States that the USA itself would not participate in an attack on Cuba and would restrain others from actions of this sort, if you would recall your fleet, this would immediately change everything. . .Then too, the question of the destruction, not only of the armaments which you call offensive, but of all other armaments as well, would look different . . .

Let us therefore show statesmanlike wisdom. I propose: We, for our part, will declare that our ships, bound for Cuba, will not carry any kind of armaments. You would declare that the United States will not invade Cuba with its forces and will not support any sort of forces which might intend to carry out an invasion of Cuba. Then the necessity for the presence of our military specialists in Cuba would disappear . . . If you did this as the first step towards the unleashing of war, well then, it is evident that nothing else is left to us but to accept this challenge of yours. If, however, you have not lost your self-control and sensibly conceive what this might lead to, then, Mr. President, we and you ought not now to pull on the ends of the rope in which you have tied the knot of war, because the more the two of us pull, the tighter that knot will be tied. And a moment may come when that knot will be tied so tight that even he who tied it will not have the strength to untie it, and then it will be necessary to cut that knot, and what that would mean is not for me to explain to you, because you yourself understand perfectly of what terrible forces our countries dispose. Consequently, if there is no intention to tighten that knot and thereby to doom the world to the catastrophe of thermonuclear war, then let us not only relax the forces pulling on the ends of the rope, let us take measures to untie that knot . . . There, Mr. President, are my thoughts, which, if you agreed with them, could put an end to that tense situation which is disturbing all peoples. These thoughts are dictated by a sincere desire to relieve the situation, to remove the threat of war.

Respectfully yours,

N. Khrushchev

Alexander Pushkin to Jacob von Heeckeren, 25 January 1837

The letter that led to the tragic death of Russia's sublime poet Pushkin. The great-grandson of Abram Hannibal, Peter the Great's black aide, Pushkin found himself in trouble with the tsars as soon as he started writing his outrageous, passionate and beautiful verses. Alexander I punished him by exiling him from Petersburg to south Russia, but even there Pushkin associated with liberals, seduced the wife of the tsar's viceroy and pursued many other love affairs until he was finally allowed home by the new tsar the grandiloquent Nicholas I, who offered to be his personal censor.

By this time Pushkin was writing his masterpiece, the verse-novel *Eugene Onegin*, and had married Natalia, a society beauty who immediately attracted the flirtatious attentions of the tsar himself (which Pushkin had to tolerate) and of a shallow French popinjay serving in the Russian Guards named Baron Charles d'Anthes. He was the adopted son and (probable) homosexual lover of the Dutch ambassador Baron Heeckeren, who paid all his expenses. Already tormented with jealousy, Pushkin, now aged thirty-seven, receives a malicious anonymous letter from 'THE SUPREME COMMANDER AND KNIGHTS OF THE MOST SERENE ORDER OF CUCKOLDS'. The proud Pushkin immediately – and probably wrongly – suspects d'Anthes of cuckolding him. The tsar tries to prevent a duel, but Pushkin, determined on satisfaction, proceeds to make confrontation inevitable with this blisteringly rude letter to Heeckeren accusing him of acting as 'the pimp of your son ... like an obscene old woman'. His son had to defend his adopted father's honour. In the subsequent duel, d'Anthes shot and killed Russia's most beloved poet. D'Anthes had to leave Russia – but later rose to a senator in France.

Baron!

Allow me to sum up what has just taken place. Your son's behaviour had long been known to me and could not be a matter of indifference to me. I contented myself with the role of an observer, entitled to intervene when I judged it proper. An incident which at any other moment would have been very disagreeable, happily supervened to get me out of the difficulty: I received anonymous letters. You know the rest: I made your son play such a pitiable role that my wife, astonished at such cowardice and servility, could not refrain from laughing, and any emotion which she had perhaps come to feel for this great and sublime passion evaporated into the calmest and most merited disgust.

I am obliged to admit, Baron, that your role has not been altogether seemly. You, the representative of a crowned head, have been paternally the pimp of your son. It appears that all his behaviour (clumsy enough, moreover) has been directed by you. It was probably you who dictated to him the sorry witticisms he has been mouthing and the twaddle he has taken upon himself to write. Like an obscene old woman, you would go and spy on my wife from every corner to speak to her of the love of your bastard, or the one so-called; and when, ill with the pox, he was confined to his home, you would say that he was dying of love for her; you would mumble: give me back my son.

You will be well aware, Baron, that after all this I cannot permit my family to have the least relation with yours. It was on this condition that I consented not to pursue this

filthy affair and not to dishonour you in the eyes of our court
and of yours, as I had the power and intention to do. I do not
care for my wife to hear again your paternal exhortations. I
cannot allow your son, after the despicable conduct he has
shown, to dare to speak to my wife, still less to mouth to
her these barrack-room calembours, and play devotion and
unhappy passion whilst he is nothing but a coward and a
scoundrel. I am thus obliged to address myself to you, to beg
you to put an end to all these goings-on, if you wish to avoid
a new scandal, from which I certainly shall not shrink.

I have the honour to be, Baron
Your most humble and obedient servant,
Alexander Pushkin

Power

Stalin to Valery Mezhlauk, April 1930

Gallows humour is Stalin's favourite kind. Here at a meeting of the Politburo, he sends a note around the table suggesting an appropriate punishment for the sins of the People's Commissar for Finance, Nikolai Bryukhanov, whom Stalin regarded as politically unreliable. His comrade Valery Mezhlauk, in charge of economic planning and a fine cartoonist, sketches this picture of the punishment – presumably to general amusement. The commissar was sacked and both Bryukhanov and Mezhlauk were later executed by Stalin.

For all new, existing and future sins, to be hung
by the balls, and if the balls are strong and
don't break, to forgive him and think correct
but if they break, then to throw him into
a river.

Churchill to Roosevelt, 20 May 1940

An appeal for help at the supreme crisis of the Second World War. Churchill has been Prime Minister for just ten days. France is defeated. Britain stands alone against Nazi Europe awaiting Hitler's invasion – and America is still neutral. Churchill asks the American President Roosevelt to sell him fifty warships to aid in defending the country, but then hears that the US ambassador to London, Joseph Kennedy, a notorious appeaser, has advised against this because Britain is about to collapse. This provokes one of Churchill's most defiant letters of British resolve:

Our intention is, whatever happens, to fight on to the end in this Island and provided we can get the help for which we ask, we hope to run them very close in the air battles in view of individual superiority. Members of the present administration would likely go down during the process should it result adversely, but in no conceivable circumstances will we consent to surrender. If members of the present administration were finished and others came to parlay amid the ruins, you must not be blind to the fact that the sole remaining bargaining counter would be the fleet, and if this country was left by the United States to its fate, no one would have the right to blame those responsible if they made the best terms they could for the surviving inhabitants. Excuse me, Mr. President, putting this nightmare bluntly. I could not answer for my successors who in utter despair and hopelessness might well have to accommodate themselves to the German will. However there is no need at present to dwell upon such ideas. Once more thanking you for your good will.

Between Richard I and Saladin, October–November 1191

Here is an attempt to negotiate a peace process by partition of the Holy Land in the late twelfth century. At this time Saladin, the Kurdish-born Islamic sultan of Syria and Egypt, has defeated the Crusader kingdom of Jerusalem and retaken the Holy City. But he has failed to retake the city of Acre where a new crusade has landed, led by the formidable Christian warrior King Richard I of England – the Lionheart. Fighting themselves to a stalemate, the two now propose to share the present state of Israel.

The climax of their negotiations? Richard proposes that his sister Joanna should marry Saladin's brother Safadin and that they rule an Islamic-Christian kingdom – together in Jerusalem under Saladin's crown. Amazingly, Saladin agrees in principle, calling Richard's bluff: unsurprisingly, his sister Joanna refused to marry a Muslim, even a king of Jerusalem. There is something very modern in their letters – in today's peace process, this time between Israel and the Palestinians, Jerusalem remains the thorniest issue. Unsurprisingly the plan failed – as have many other plans to make peace in the Middle East.

Richard to Saladin

Men of ours and of yours have died, the country is in ruins, and events have entirely escaped anyone's control. Do you not believe that it is enough? As far as we are concerned, there are only three subjects of discord: Jerusalem, the True Cross, and territory. As for Jerusalem, it is our place of worship and we will never agree to renounce it, even if we have to fight to the last man. As territory, all we want is that the land west of the Jordan be ceded to us. As for the Cross, for you it is merely a piece of wood, whereas for us its value is inestimable. Let the Sultan give it to us, and let us put an end to this exhausting struggle.

Saladin to Richard

Jerusalem is holy to us as well as to you, and more so, seeing it is the scene of our Prophet's journey, and the place where our people must assemble at the Last Day. Think not that we shall go back therefrom, or that we can be compliant in this matter. And as for the land, it was ours to begin with, and you invaded it: nor [would you have taken it] but for the feebleness of the Muslims who then had it; and so long as this war lasts God will not permit you to set up a stone in it. And as for the Cross, our holding it is a point of vantage, nor can we surrender it except for some benefit of Islam.

Arthur James Balfour to Lord Rothschild, 2 November 1917

The letter that changed the Middle East. Ever since the Jewish Temple was destroyed by Titus Caesar in AD 70, Jews had revered Zion and dreamed of a return to Jerusalem. In the late nineteenth century vicious persecutions in Russia – home to six million Jews – and anti-Semitic attacks spanning France to Austria, inspired a modern Zionist movement. Even before the First World War, many leading British statesmen were sympathetic to the history and the plight of the Jews, but the circumstances of the war made it possible. In 1917 British troops were poised to invade Palestine, which had been ruled by the Ottoman sultans for four centuries, but the British were also desperate, after years of bloody stalemate on the Western Front, to keep both Russia and the US in the war. Both contained large Jewish populations.

Foreign Secretary Balfour writes a letter – 'the Balfour Declaration' – which promises the creation of a Jewish national home in the Holy Land without prejudicing the rights of the Arab population already living there. It takes the form of a public letter to one of the leaders of the Jewish community, Walter Rothschild, 2nd Baron, head of the Zionist Federation. In 1948, the state of Israel was created.

Dear Lord Rothschild,

I have much pleasure in conveying to you, on behalf of His Majesty's Government, the following declaration of sympathy with Jewish Zionist aspirations which has been submitted to, and approved by, the Cabinet:

> *His Majesty's Government view with favour the establishment in Palestine of a national home for the Jewish people, and will use their best endeavours to facilitate the achievement of this object, it being clearly understood that nothing shall be done which may prejudice the civil and religious rights of existing non-Jewish communities in Palestine, or the rights and political status enjoyed by Jews in any other country.*

I should be grateful if you would bring this declaration to the knowledge of the Zionist Federation.

Yours,

Arthur James Balfour

George Bush to Bill Clinton, 20 January 1993

Here's a letter that defines big-hearted statesmanship in our meanspirited era. George H.W. Bush was one of the best qualified US presidents of modern times and the very definition of an American upper-class gentleman. A war hero pilot who had been shot down in the Second World War, he made a fortune in oil then was elected to the House of Representatives before serving as ambassador to the UN, envoy to China and director of the CIA before becoming Ronald Reagan's vice president and succeeding him as the 41st president. Neither a brilliant statesman nor a charismatic visionary, he was a somewhat uninspiring if steady servant of the nation. He was bemused and alarmed by the fall of the Soviet Union, and rather late to adapt to the reality of newly independent states like Russia and Ukraine. But he reacted to the Iraqi dictator Saddam Hussein's invasion of Kuwait by putting together a coalition that liberated the country and hobbled the tyrant while leaving him in power. Faced with the brash energy of the young governor of Arkansas, Bill Clinton, he looked old-fashioned and out of touch in a bruising campaign.

Yet on losing his beloved presidency he sits and writes this charming and magnanimous letter which he leaves on his desk in the Oval Office for his rival Clinton. From the last of the old-fashioned war-generation leaders, here is a masterclass in dutiful service, personal decency and respect for your opponents. This is how power should change hands in a liberal democracy.

Dear Bill,

When I walked into this office just now I felt the same sense of wonder and respect that I felt four years ago. I know you will feel that, too.

I wish you great happiness here. I never felt the loneliness some Presidents have described.

There will be very tough times, made even more difficult by criticism you may not think is fair. I'm not a very good one to give advice; but just don't let the critics discourage you or push you off course.

You will be our President when you read this note. I wish you well. I wish your family well.

Your success is now our country's success. I am rooting hard for you.

Good luck –

George

Niccolò Machiavelli to Francesco Vettori,
3 August 1514

The Italian politician Niccolò Machiavelli was also a wry observer of human nature. He was at the peak of his professional powers between 1498 and 1512, when he served as Secretary to the Second Chancery of the Republic of Florence. Losing favour after a coup the following year, he was arrested and tortured, finally being released to his estate where he relaxed, walked, read poetry and wrote his most famous work, The Prince which, using the rise and fall of his contemporary Cesare Borgia, analysed the conduct of politicians with amoral realism: 'Whether it be better to be loved than feared or feared than loved? One should wish to be both not because it is difficult to unite them in one person, it is much safer to be feared than loved.' His letters, often to his friend Francesco Vettori, Florentine ambassador in Rome, are not always political. In this one, dated 5 January 1514, he recommends the pleasures of love in all its varieties, straight or gay – a charming definition of rather unMachiavellian tolerance: 'He who is deemed wise during the day will never be considered crazy at night, and he who is esteemed a respectable man, and is worthy, whatever he does to lighten his heart and live happily renders him honour, not blame. Rather being called a bugger or a whoremongerer, one says he is a man of broad interests, easygoing, and a good fellow.'

In this letter, written a few months later, he writes beautifully about falling in love at the age of fifty:

My friend . . . I have encountered a creature so gracious, so delicate . . . that I cannot praise her so much or love her so much that she would not deserve more. I ought to tell you with what nets of gold, spread among flowers, woven by Venus, so pleasant and easy that a villainous heart might have broken . . . You should not believe that Love in order to take me has used ordinary methods, because knowing they would not have been enough for him, he used extraordinary ones of which I knew nothing and from which I could not protect myself. May it be enough for you that already near fifty years neither do these suns harm me, nor do rough, roads tire me, nor dark hours of night frighten me. Everything seems to me level and all her desires . . . I adapt myself . . . I feel in it such sweetness both through what that face so soft and wonderful brings me, and also through having laid aside the memory of all my troubles, that for anything in the world, being able to free myself I would not wish it. I have abandoned then the thoughts of affairs great and serious . . . they are all turned into soft conversations for which I thank Venus. So if it occurs to you to write anything about the lady write it . . . Farewell.

Henry VII to his 'good friends', July 1485

It looks like a crazy adventure. On 7 August 1485, Henry Tudor and a small army of two thousand French mercenaries land in Wales, determined to seize the kingdom of England from King Richard III. Henry's claim to the throne is through his mother Lady Margaret Beaufort, the great-granddaughter of John of Gaunt, fourth son of Edward III; he is also descended from a minor Welsh soldier, Owen Tudor, who had married Henry V's widow. However tenuous this connection may be, many better claimants are dead, and everyone knows that Richard III has usurped the throne from his own nephews: the two young princes have vanished, in the summer of 1483, murdered on Richard's orders. The taint of regicide and infanticide is pungent.

A year earlier, Henry Tudor had attempted an invasion which had failed. Now he issues this open letter to potential followers among the noble magnates. The timing is perfect – rarely has a political letter been so successful. As he marches into England, more and more grandees support him.

At the Battle of Bosworth Field on 22 August, various key magnates, above all the Stanleys, switch sides. Richard loses the battle, killed in the field. The penniless half-Welsh claimant, who lacks even the proper clothes to wear at his own court, has founded the Tudor dynasty.

Right trusty, worshipful and honourable good friends, and our allies, I greet you well. Being given to understand your good devoir and intent to advance me to the furtherance of my rightful claim due and lineal inheritance of the crown, and for the just depriving of that homicide and unnatural tyrant which now unjustly bears dominion over you, I give you to understand that no Christian heart can be more full of joy upon the instance of your sure advertise what powers ye will make ready and what captains and leaders you get to conduct, be prepared to pass over the sea with such forces as my friends are preparing for me. And if you have such good speed and success as I wish, according to your desire, I shall be ever most forward to remember and wholly to requite this your great and most loving kindness in my just quarrel.

Given under our signet,

HR

John Adams to Thomas Jefferson, 20 February 1801

The handover of power is a test of every system – but even when it runs smoothly it is often extremely awkward. John Adams was the second US President, whose administration had been something of a mess. He was also the first president to live in the White House. His vice president had been his old comrade Thomas Jefferson with whom he enjoyed a close and long but touchy relationship. After the 1800 election, when Adams sees his party wiped out, he unworthily tries to stack governmental appointments against the incoming President Jefferson, who denounces this perfidy. Hence Adams's letter is frostily concerned not with the handover of the sacred altar of democracy but with the correct number of horses. After a long sulk on Adams's part and two successful terms of the Jeffersonian presidency, they became friends again in 1811.

Sir

In order to save you the trouble and Expence of purchasing Horses and Carriages, which will not be necessary, I have to inform you that I shall leave in the stables of the United States seven Horses and two Carriages with Harness the Property of the United States. These may not be suitable for you: but they will certainly save you a considerable Expence as they belong to the stud of the President's Household.

I have the Honor to be with great respect, Sir, your most obedient and humble Servant.

Between the Duke of Marlborough, Queen Anne and Sarah, Duchess of Marlborough, 13 August 1704

A triangle of power, victory and love all recorded in intimate letters. Anne, daughter of James II, was the needy, awkward Protestant queen, an unlikely monarch to oversee the defeat of Louis XIV's attempt to dominate Europe. Anne was tormented by ill health and obesity, a condition exacerbated by the misery of seventeen unsuccessful pregnancies with her husband Prince Georg of Denmark.

The second of this trio was the general John Churchill. On the succession of James II in 1685, he initially backed the king but he sympathised with Protestant Whiggery instead of James' Catholic absolutism. In 1688, when William of Orange (who was married to Mary, another of James II's daughters), landed in England, Churchill supported the Glorious Revolution – and was rewarded with the earldom of Marlborough.

Meeting the strong-willed Sarah Jennings, aged fifteen, at court, Marlborough fell in love and married her just as Sarah became best friends with Anne, now heir to the throne. Anne looked to Sarah for emotional sustenance, writing her such passionate letters that Sarah later accused her of lesbianism. 'I hope I shall get a moment or two to be with my dear,' writes Anne to Sarah. 'That I may have one dear embrace which I long for more than I can express.' To ensure secrecy in their letter-writing, they called each other Mrs Morley and Mrs Freeman.

In 1702, when Anne succeeds to the throne, Britain is fighting France and Marlborough, now captain-general, wins an unbroken series of victories. Here, after Blenheim, his greatest victory, he writes to Sarah to tell the queen instead of writing to Anne directly, consolidating Sarah's importance. Marlborough received a dukedom and Blenheim Palace, but ultimately, Mrs Morley and Mrs Freeman fell out viciously, contributing to Marlborough's fall and the end of the war.

I have not time to say more, but beg you will give my duty to the Queen and let her know her army has had a glorious victory. M Tallard [Marshal of France] and two other generals are in my coach and I am following the rest. The bearer, my aide de camp Colonel Parke, will give her an account of what has passed. I shall do it in a day or two by another more at large.

Donald J. Trump to Kim Jong Un, 24 May 2018

A letter characteristic of the world-changing style of President Donald Trump. Considering himself to be a global dealmaker, if only trained by his experiences in New York real estate and US reality television, Trump believes that his personal diplomacy at summit meetings can achieve deals unreachable by more conventional politicians.

In early 2018, he is convinced that if he is able to meet with the youthful North Korean dictator Kim Jong Un, he can solve the dangerous problem of the nuclear arsenal built by the Kim dynasty to protect their seventy-year rule. When North Korean negotiators become hostile, Trump turns to the old-fashioned diplomatic letter, a form that may appeal to the rigid Stalinist formality of the dynasty. But its tone is typical of this presidency. Highly Trumpian in its bombastic swagger, theatrical menace and plangent sentimentality, it is perhaps the first letter in which a US president so brazenly trumpets his nuclear power and threatens to unleash its apocalyptic force. The letter works. Kim replies with his own formal letter of reconciliation.

The spectacular summit was held in Singapore on 12 June, but the real denuclearisation of Korea would be harder to achieve. Nonetheless, this exchange of letters is typical of a strange time in world affairs.

The White House
Washington DC
May 24 2018

His Excellency Kim Jong Un
Chairman of the State Affairs Commission of the Democratic People's Republic of Korea

Dear Mr Chairman:

We greatly appreciate your time, patience, and effort with respect to our recent negotiations and discussions relative to a summit long sought by both parties . . . I was very much looking forward to being there with you. Sadly, based on the tremendous anger and open hostility displayed in your most recent statement, I feel it is inappropriate, at this time, to have this long-planned meeting . . . You talk about your nuclear capabilities, but ours are so massive and powerful that I pray to God they will never have to be used . . . If you change your mind having to do with this most important summit, please do not hesitate to call me or write. The world, and North Korea in particular, has lost a great opportunity for lasting peace and great prosperity and wealth. This missed opportunity is a truly sad moment in history.

Sincerely yours, Donald J Trump.
President of the United States of America

Downfall

Abd al-Rahman III to his sons, AD 961

Abd al-Rahman was the most magnificent of the Arab rulers of al-Andalus, the Muslim kingdom of Spain. He was descended from Abd al-Rahman I, the Ummayad prince who had escaped from Baghdad, ruled by his enemies the Abbasid caliphs, travelled in disguise across Africa and then founded his own realm in Spain. After his death the kingdom had declined until the succession of Abd al-Rahman III in 912. A superb general and merciless politician, he embarked on decades of war to defeat all rivals, Muslim and Christian, and dominate Iberia to such an extent that in 929, he declared himself Caliph – Commander of the Faithful – in a letter to the world that damned the Abbasid caliphs of Baghdad as fakes: 'We are the most worthy to fulfil our right, and the most entitled to complete our good fortune, and to put on the clothing granted by the nobility of God, because of the favour which He has shown us, and the renown which He has given us, and the power to which He has raised us ... We have decided that the acclamation should be to us as Commander of the Faithful ... Everyone who calls himself by this name apart from ourselves is arrogating it to himself and trespassing upon it ...'

As the seventy-year-old caliph lies dying in 961, the most glorious monarch of his time, he writes this letter, supposedly left for his successor, which is the very definition of humility from the most powerful of rulers: in fifty years of victory, just fourteen days of pleasure.

I have now reigned above fifty years in victory or peace, beloved by my subjects, dreaded by my enemies, and respected by my allies. Riches and honours, power and pleasure, have waited on my call, nor does any earthly blessing appear to have been wanting to my felicity. In this situation, I have diligently numbered the days of pure and genuine happiness which have fallen to my lot: they amount to FOURTEEN:—O man! place not thy confidence in this present world!

Simon Bar Kokhba to Yeshua, c.AD 135

In 130, Roman Emperor Hadrian visited Jerusalem, in ruins since the destruction of the Temple and city by Titus in 70, and decided to re-found it as a pagan city, named after himself and featuring a temple of Jupiter on the site of the Holy of Holies. In 132, a mysterious leader calling himself the Prince of Israel led a powerful rebellion that swiftly destroyed two Roman legions. This was the start of a new Jewish revolt under the command of the prince whose name was probably Shimon ben Kosiba, though his followers hailed him as Simon Bar Kokhba, Son of the Star.

Hadrian rushed reinforcements to crush this new state of Israel but it took three tough years of fighting: finally in 135, Simon was besieged and killed in his fortress of Betar; Hadrian's revenge on the Jews was almost genocidal – the sources claim 500,000 were slaughtered; Jerusalem was renamed Aelia Capitolina after Hadrian's family and became a pagan city; Judea was renamed Palestina. Amazingly in 1960, fifteen of Simon's letters were found in a Judean cave and here is one. Archaeologists debate the meaning of the word 'destroy' which is damaged and hard to decipher: it was thought at one point that S.B.K. was telling Yeshua to protect the Galileans but now it seems he was telling him to do something bad to them. This correspondence probably dates from the last days of the revolt as the prince struggles to keep control over his diminishing forces. The downfall of the last Jewish state (until 1948) is close.

From Shimon ben Kosiba to Yeshua ben Galgoula and the men of the fortress. Peace to you. Heaven is my witness against me that unless you destroy the Galileans who are with you down to the last man, I shall, as I did to ben Aphul, put fetters on your feet.

Ammurapi to the king of Alashiya,
C.1190 BC

Around 1190 BC, an army of seafaring marauders attacked a prosperous Syrian city, Ugarit, which had close relations with other powers of the late Bronze Age world: Egypt to the south and the Hittites to the north. As the marauders attack, the king of Ugarit, Ammurapi appeals to his Alashiyan (Cypriot) neighbour. We still do not know the identity of the aggressors, so they are known as the Sea Peoples. In this letter, Ammurapi recounts the beginning of the destruction of his kingdom. Even reading it three thousand years later, its desperation is tangible – and no wonder. The Sea Peoples destroyed many of the empires of the day.

My father, behold, the enemy's ships came [here]; my cities were burned, and they did evil things in my country. Does not my father know that all my troops and chariots are in the Land of Hatti, and all my ships are in the Land of Lukka? . . . Thus, the country is abandoned to itself. May my father know it: the seven ships of the enemy that came here inflicted much damage upon us.

Aurangzeb to his son Muhammad Azam Shah, 1707

A letter of humility before death, from a man of intolerant power. Aurangzeb 'the world-seizer' was the last great Mughal emperor of India. He was born the third son of Shah Jahan, builder of the Taj Mahal. After a struggle for power in which he brutally executed all his rival brothers, he humiliated his father, then imposed a severe Islamic regime on the multi-religious, multi-ethnic empire, dangerously weakening it. After crushing rebellions from Hindus and Sikhs, Aurangzeb lies dying, filled with regrets and doubts, and writes this to his son.

Health to thee! My heart is near thee. Old age is arrived: weakness subdues me, and strength has forsaken all my members. I came a stranger into this world, and a stranger I depart. I know nothing of myself, what I am, and for what I am destined. The instant which passed in power, hath left only sorrow behind it. I have not been the guardian and protector of the empire. My valuable time has been passed vainly. I had a patron in my own dwelling [he probably means his conscience], but his glorious light was unseen by my dim sight. Life is not lasting; there is no vestige of departed breath, and all hopes from futurity are lost. The fever has left me, but nothing of me remains but skin and bone. My son [Kaum Buksh], though gone towards Beejapore, is still near; and thou, my son, art yet nearer. The worthy of esteem, Shaw Aulum, is far distant; and my grandson [Azeem Ooshawn], by the orders of God, is arrived near Hindustan. The camp and followers, helpless and alarmed, are, like myself, full of affliction, restless as the quicksilver. Separated from their lord, they know not if they have a master or not.

I brought nothing into this world, and, except the infirmities of man, carry nothing out. I have a dread for my salvation, and with what torments I may be punished. Though I have strong reliance on the mercies and bounty of God, yet, regarding my actions, fear will not quit me; but, when I am gone, reflection will not remain. Come what may, I have launched my vessel to the waves. Though Providence will protect the camp, yet, regarding appearances, the endeavours of my sons are indispensably incumbent. Give my last prayers to my grandson [Bedar Bakht], whom I cannot see, but the desire affects me. The Begum [his daughter] appears afflicted; but God is the only judge of hearts. The foolish thoughts of women produce nothing but disappointment. Farewell! farewell! farewell!

Bolívar to José Flores, 9 November 1830

All political careers end in failure but this is political despondency. Simón Bolívar has liberated half of South America from Spanish rule and served as President of Gran Colombia, dictator of Peru and much else, but his career ends catastrophically in the collapse of his authority and the state he has created. He retires on 20 January 1830. After the assassination of his closest ally, Marshal José de Sucre, he is in despair. Already dying, he writes to President Flores of Ecuador: 'Avenge Sucre's murder . . . then get out while you can.' Soon after delivering this damning assessment of South America's future, he died of tuberculosis, aged just forty-five.

Use the past to predict the future. You know that I have ruled for twenty years, and I have derived from these only a few sure conclusions: . . . 1. America is ungovernable; 2. He who serves a revolution ploughs the sea; 3. all one can do in America is leave it; 4. the country is bound to fall into unimaginable chaos, after which it will pass into the hands of an indistinguishable string of tyrants of every colour and races; 5. once we are devoured by all manner of crime and reduced to a frenzy of violence, no one – not even the Europeans – will want to subjugate us; 6. and, finally, if mankind could revert to its primitive state, it would be here in America, in her final hour.

Goodbye

Leonard Cohen to Marianne Ihlen, July 2016

Saying goodbye is one of the arts of letter-writing. No other singer-songwriter between the 1960s and the start of the twenty-first century was such a master of words, as well as music, as Leonard Cohen. He regarded himself primarily as a poet, but it is the lyrics and songs that are his masterpieces, many of them based on his love affairs with women who became his muses – songs such as 'Suzanne' and 'Nancy' and the 'Sisters of Mercy', but no one inspired him more than Marianne Ihlen, a young Norwegian who in 1960 moved to live with Cohen on the island of Hydra in Greece. She inspired many of his greatest songs such as 'Bird on the Wire' and above all 'So Long, Marianne'.

After they broke up in the late 1960s, she married and moved to Oslo. Many years later, in 2016, she was diagnosed with leukaemia. She was failing fast in hospital and expected to die soon. On 1 July she asks her close friend Jan Christian Mollestad to notify Leonard Cohen who, at eighty-two, is still singing and writing though he too is ill. Jan sends a letter that night to Cohen telling him Marianne has 'only a few days to live' and ending 'I hope you read this in time to reach her. And I hope you don't think I am interfering. I just pass on Marianne's deep love for you.' Jan does not have much hope that he will receive a reply from Leonard Cohen but at dawn, after a sleepless night, he finds this beautiful letter. Jan reads her the letter. 'These seven sentences from Leonard – this sign of everlasting affection – gave Marianne a new level of peace.' She falls into coma a day later, dying two days afterwards. Leonard Cohen himself died that November. Maybe he saw Marianne 'down the road' . . .

Dearest Marianne,
I'm just a little behind you, close enough to take your hand.
This old body has given up, as yours has too, and the
eviction notice is on its way any day now.
I've never forgotten your love and your beauty. But you

know that. I don't have to say more.
Safe travels, old friend.
See you down the road.
Endless love
and gratitude,
Leonard

'Henriette' to Giacomo Casanova, autumn 1749

This is the classic end-of-the-affair letter. The adventurer Giacomo Casanova is celebrated as a prolific lover, who commented 'I have loved women to a frenzy', but he was also variously a librarian, spy, occultist, sponger, fraudster and fantasist – as well as a wonderful letter-writer and memoirist. His first sexual adventure with a pair of sisters launched him on a career as a womaniser but he was never as cold-hearted as he claimed with his 132 paramours, and he loved intelligent women: 'conversation is two-thirds of pleasure', he said.

Casanova receives this letter from the one woman he may have truly loved: the pseudonymous Henriette, whom he met in early 1749 in Parma. Freespirited and a brilliant conversationalist with superb taste, 'those who believe a woman is incapable of making a man happy twenty-four hours a day have never known a Henriette'. She was probably a Provençal noblewoman trapped in an unhappy marriage; but it is she, rather than he, who eventually ends it, leaving him a gift of five hundred louis and scratching with a diamond on the window: 'You will forget Henriette too'.

Her letter is utterly charming – 'Let us swear never to forget one another'. One presumes she is returning to her boring husband. As so often in such scenarios, the writer swears never to have another illicit affair, but wishes the heartbroken Casanova many other Henriettes: 'you will love again.' But he knows it will never be the same – there is only one Henriette in a life.

They did meet again – in 1769, when she was fifty-one. When

Casanova initially failed to recognise her, she commented – 'Plumpness has altered my physiognomy.' Her true identity is still unknown.

It is I, dearest and best friend, who have been compelled to abandon you, but do not let your grief be increased by any thought of my sorrow. Let us be wise enough to suppose that we have had a happy dream, and not to complain of destiny, for never did so beautiful a dream last so long! Let us be proud of the consciousness that for three months we gave one another the most perfect felicity. Few human beings can boast of so much! Let us swear never to forget one another, and to often remember the happy hours of our love, in order to renew them in our souls, which, although divided, will enjoy them as acutely as if our hearts were beating one against the other. Do not make any enquiries about me, and if chance should let you know who I am, forget it for ever. I feel certain that you will be glad to hear that I have arranged my affairs so well that I shall, for the remainder of my life, be as happy as I can possibly be without you, dear friend, by my side. I do not know who you are, but I am certain that no one in the world knows you better than I do. I shall not have another lover as long as I live, but I do not wish you to imitate me. On the contrary I hope that you will love again, and I trust that a good fairy will bring along your path another Henriette.

Farewell . . . farewell.

Churchill to his wife Clementine, 17 July 1915

As the world careened into the First World War in 1914, Winston Churchill, aged forty-one, was serving in the Cabinet as First Lord of the Admiralty in the charge of the fleet of the world's paramount sea power. Like everyone else in Europe, he was horrified by the purblind, feverish stagger into war, writing to his wife Clementine in July 1914: 'I cannot feel that we in this island are in any serious degree responsible for the wave of madness which has swept the mind of Christendom. No one can measure the consequences. I wondered whether those stupid Kings and Emperors could not assemble together and revivify kingship by saving the nations from hell but we all drift on in a kind of dull cataleptic trance.' Once the initial German attacks against France and Russia had failed to knock them out of the war, the war descended into a murderous trench warfare which Churchill tried to solve in an imaginative way by suggesting an attack on the weakest link among Germany's allies, the Ottoman Empire, thereby relieving pressure on the Russians and hopefully capturing Istanbul. This was a sensible idea, but it was appallingly executed, and it became the disastrous Gallipoli campaign. Churchill was removed from the Admiralty and demoted. He resigned in November 1915 to serve in the trenches as a lieutenant-colonel, returning to the government in July 1917.

It is during his political limbo preparing to enlist that he writes this letter to Clementine to be opened 'in the event of my death'. Mentioning his son Randolph as his heir, Churchill treats Clementine with a characteristic combination of political pragmatism, bumptious self-confidence, romantic love, and a chivalric even spiritual open-mindedness, especially his promise that 'if there is anywhere else I shall be on the lookout for you.'

In the event of my death.

I am anxious that you should get hold of all my papers, especially those which refer to my Admiralty administration. I have appointed you my sole literary executor . . . There is no hurry; but some day I should like the truth to be known. Randolph will carry on the lamp. Do not grieve for me too much. I am a spirit confident of my rights. Death is only an incident, and not the most important which happens to us in this state of being. On the whole, especially since I met you my darling one, I have been happy, and you have you taught me how noble a woman's heart can be. If there is anywhere else I shall be on the lookout for you. Meanwhile look forward, feel free, rejoice in life, cherish the children, guard my memory. God bless you. Good-bye. W

Nikolai Bukharin to Stalin, 10 December 1937

A letter of devotion and submission from a man to his killer. This is one of the strangest letters in this book, both heartbreaking and horrific, reflecting the bizarre murderous frenzy of the Great Terror in Soviet Russia. In the late 1920s, Stalin and Nikolai Bukharin had been intimate friends and political allies in ruling the Soviet Union. Their wives were friends, their families ran in and out of each other's houses. Bukharin was an intellectual who had been described by Lenin as 'the darling of the Party'. But in 1929, Stalin turned against Bukharin who in turn plotted with Stalin's enemies and continued to be friends with Stalin's wife Nadezhda. She committed suicide in 1932. In 1934, Bukharin remarried a young and pretty daughter of another Party leader.

During the thirties, Stalin toyed with Bukharin until 1936 when he launched a purge of the Bolshevik leadership, orchestrating the destruction of his former friend. The Terror intensified as Stalin arranged the arrest, torture and execution of around a million people. Finally, Bukharin was arrested and forced to confess to crimes he did not commit. Knowing he is likely to be shot by the remorseless Stalin he writes a final letter from prison. Yet as a Bolshevik, devoted to the Marxist–Leninist mission before everything, even his own life, he expresses devotion to Stalin – his friend Koba – and to the Communist Party, and admires the big idea of a brutal purge. Desperate and feverish, the letter is extraordinary in its mixture of love and humiliation – and Bukharin's readiness to die for the Party confessing crimes he never committed. Stalin wanted Bukharin to die. He was executed after his public trial on 15 March 1938. Stalin is said to have kept this letter in his desk for the rest of his life.

VERY SECRET

PERSONAL

Request no one be allowed to *read* this letter without the
express permission of I.V. Stalin.

Iosif Vissarionovich:

This is perhaps the last letter I shall write to you before
my death. That's why, though I am a prisoner, I ask you
to permit me to write this letter without resorting to
officialese, all the more so since I am writing this letter to
you alone: the very fact of its existence or nonexistence will
remain entirely in your hands.

I've come to the last page of my drama and perhaps of my
very life. I agonised over whether I should pick up pen and
paper – as I write this, I am shuddering all over from disquiet
and from a thousand emotions stirring within me, and I can
hardly control myself. But precisely because I have so little
time left, I want to *take my leave* of you in advance, before
it's too late, before my hand ceases to write, before my eyes
close, while my brain somehow still functions.

In order to avoid any misunderstandings, I will say to you
from the outset that, as far as *the world at large* (society) is
concerned: a) I have no intention of recanting anything I've
written down [confessed]; b) In *this* sense (or in connection
with this), I have no intention of asking you or pleading
with you for anything that might derail my case from the
direction in which it is heading. But I am writing to you for
your *personal* information. I cannot leave this life without
writing to you these last lines because I am in the grip of
torments which you should know about . . .

There is something *great and bold about the political idea*
of a general purge. It is a) connected with the pre-war
situation and b) connected with the transition to democracy.
This purge encompasses 1) the guilty; 2) persons under

suspicion; and 3) persons potentially under suspicion. This business could not have been managed without me. Some are neutralised one way, others in another way, and a third group in yet another way. What serves as a guarantee for all is the fact that people inescapably talk about each other and in doing so arouse an *everlasting* distrust in each other . . . In this way, the leadership is bringing about a *full guarantee* for itself.

For God's sake, don't think that I am engaging here in reproaches, even in my inner thoughts. I wasn't born yesterday. I know all too well that *great* plans, *great* ideas, and *great* interests take precedence over everything, and I know that it would be petty for me to place the question of my own person *on a par with the universal-historical* tasks resting, first and foremost on your shoulders . . .

Permit me, finally, to move on to my last, minor, requests.

a) it would be a thousand times easier for me *to die* than to go through the coming trial: I simply don't know how I'll be able to control myself – you know my nature: I am not an enemy either of the party or of the USSR, and I'll do all within my powers [to serve my party's cause], but, under such circumstances, my powers are minimal, and heavy emotions rise up in my soul . . .

b) If I'm to receive the death sentence, then I implore you beforehand, I entreat you, by all that you hold dear, not to have me shot. Let me drink poison in my cell instead. (Let me have morphine so that I can fall asleep and never wake up.) For me, this point is extremely important. I don't know what words I should summon up in order to entreat you to grant me this as an act of charity. After all, politically, it won't really matter, and, besides, no one will know a thing about it. But let me spend my last moments as I wish. Have pity on me! Surely you'll understand – knowing me as well

as you do. Sometimes I look death openly in the face, just as
I know very well that I am capable of brave deeds. At other
times, I, ever the same person, find myself in such disarray
that I am drained of all strength. So if the verdict is death, let
me have a cup of morphine. I *implore* you . . .

c) I ask you to allow me to bid farewell to my wife and
son. No need for me to say goodbye to my daughter. I feel
sorry for her. It will be too painful for her. It will also be
too painful for Nadya [Bukharin's first wife] and my father.
Anyuta, on the other hand, is young. She will survive. I
would like to exchange a few last words with her. I would
like permission to meet her *before* the trial. My argument
is as follows: if my family sees what I *confessed* to, they
might commit suicide from sheer unexpectedness. I must
somehow prepare them for it. It seems to me that this is in
the interests of the case and its official interpretation.

d) If, contrary to expectation, my life is to be spared, I
would like to request (though I would first have to discuss it
with my wife) . . . That I be exiled to America for x number
of years . . . But if there is the slightest doubt in your mind,
then exile me to a camp in *Pechora* or *Kolyma*, even for 25
years . . .

Iosif Vissarionovich! In me you have lost one of your most
capable generals, one who is genuinely devoted to you. But
that is all past . . . I am preparing myself mentally to depart
from this vale of tears, and there is nothing in me towards
all of you, towards the party and the cause, but a great and
boundless love. I am doing everything that is humanly
possible and impossible. I have written to you about all this.
I have crossed all the t's and dotted all the i's. I have done
all this *in advance*, since I have no idea at all what condition I
shall be in tomorrow and the day after tomorrow, etc. Being
a neurasthenic, I shall perhaps feel such universal apathy
that I won't be able to even so much as move my finger.

But now, in spite of a headache and with tears in my eyes,
I am writing. My conscience is clear before you now, Koba.
I ask you one final time for your forgiveness (only in your
heart, not otherwise). For that reason I embrace you in my
mind. Farewell forever and remember kindly your wretched
   N. Bukharin

Franz Kafka to Max Brod, June 1924

Franz Kafka wrote of alienation, secrecy and persecution by sinister bur-
eaucracies, and his last letter to his best friend Max Brod displayed all
the themes of his works. Born in Prague, Kafka was a Jewish insurance
official turned novelist who produced masterpieces such as *The Trial*
and *The Castle* and was an obsessional womaniser, yet simultaneously
he was tormented by the fear of literary and sexual failure. He therefore
destroyed 90 per cent of what he wrote. While he is dying of tuberculosis, he tells Brod to destroy all of his works, which he believed would
ruin his literary reputation. Brod chose to ignore his friend's request
and between 1925 and 1933 published the work that spawned the term
'Kafkaesque'.

Dear Max,
   My last request: Everything I leave behind me . . . in the
way of notebooks, manuscripts, letters, my own and other
people's, sketches and so on, is to be burned unread and to the
last page, as well as all writings of mine or notes which either
you may have or other people, from whom you are to beg
them in my name. Letters which are not handed over to you
should at least be faithfully burned by those who have them.
   Yours,
   Franz Kafka

Walter Raleigh to his wife Bess, 8 December 1603

There is a certain sort of letter by a person who, facing death in the morning, nonetheless manages to write in a fearlessly jaunty tone, and this is one of the best. On 17 November 1603, Sir Walter Raleigh was sentenced to death for treason, thanks to his involvement in the 'Main Plot' against the new king James I. The night before his execution he writes this letter to Bess, which contains matter-of-fact financial details, expressions of love for his wife and son, and reflections on death with sentiments of swashbuckling courage and unbearable sadness.

A paragon of his age, Raleigh was a favourite of Elizabeth I – dashingly handsome, an adventurer, privateer and admiral who founded the first colony in North America, raided Spanish possessions in Latin America and co-commanded attacks on Spain itself. He was not just a man of action but of letters too, an acclaimed poet and historian, and a chemist. The morning after this letter was written, Raleigh was taken out to be beheaded then reprieved by the king at the last moment, but kept in the Tower of London for over a decade – until 1616 – giving him the chance to write a history of the world and many other works. He persuaded the king to release him to go off in search of El Dorado (a legendary city of gold that he believed awaited discovery in today's Venezuela). His expedition discovered no gold, which infuriated the king's Spanish allies. The Spanish ambassador demanded Raleigh's head. He was finally executed in 1618. Bess was said to have had Walter's head embalmed and to have carried it round with her until her own death in 1647.

Winchester, 8 December 1603

You shall now receive (my dear wife) my last words in these my last lines. My love I send you, that you may keep it when I am dead, and my counsel that you may remember it when I am no more. I would not by my will present you with sorrows (dear Bess). Let them go to the grave with me and be buried in the dust. And seeing that it is not the will of God that I should see you any more in this life, bear it patiently, and with a heart like thy self.

First, I send you all the thanks which my heart can conceive, or my words can express for your many travails, and care taken for me, which, though they have not taken effect as you wished, yet my debt to you is not the less: but pay it I never shall in this world.

Secondly, I beseech you for the love you bear me living, do not hide your self many days, but by your travails seek to help your miserable fortunes and the right of your poor child. Thy mourning cannot avail me, I am but dust.

Thirdly, you shall understand, that my land was conveyed bona fide to my child: the writings were drawn at midsummer twelve months. My honest cousin Brett can testify so much, and Dalberry, too, can remember somewhat therein. And I trust that my blood will quench their malice that have thus cruelly murthered me: and that they will not seek also to kill thee and thine with extreme poverty. To what friend to direct thee I know not, for all mine have left me in the true time of trial. And I plainly perceive that my death was determined from the first day.

Most sorry I am, God knows, that being thus surprised with death I can leave you in no better estate. God is my witness I meant you all my office of wines or all that I could have purchased by selling it, half of my stuff, and all my jewels, but some of it for the boy. But God hath prevented all my resolutions, and even great God that ruleth all in all. But if you live free from want, care for no more, for the rest is but vanity.

Love God, and begin betimes to repose your self upon him, and therein shall you find true and lasting riches, and endless comfort: for the rest when you have travailed and wearied your thoughts over all sorts of worldly cogitations, you shall but sit down by sorrow in the end. Teach your son also to love and fear God whilst he is yet young, that the fear of God may grow with him, and the same God will be a husband to you, and a father to him; a husband and a father which cannot be taken from you.

Baylie oweth me 200 pounds, and Adrian Gilbert 600. In Jersey I also have much owing me besides. The arrearages of the wines will pay my debts. And howsoever you do, for my soul's sake, pay all poor men. When I am gone, no doubt you shall be sought for by many, for the world thinks that I was very rich. But take heed of the pretences of men, and their affections, for they last not, but in honest and worthy men, and no greater misery can befall you in this life, than to become a prey, and afterwards to be despised. I speak not this (God knows) to dissuade you from marriage, for it will be best for you, both in respect of the world and of God.

As for me, I am no more yours, nor you mine. Death hath cut us asunder and God hath divided me from the world, and you from me. Remember your poor child for his father's sake, who chose you, and loved you in his happiest times.

Get those letters (if it be possible) which I writ to the Lords, wherein I sued for my life. God is my witness, it was for you and yours that I desired life. But it is true that I disdained my self for begging of it. For know it (my dear wife) that your son is the son of a true man, and one who in his own respect despiseth death and all his misshapen and ugly formes.

I cannot write much. God he knows how hardly I steal this time while others sleep, and it is also time that I should separate my thoughts from the world. Beg my dead body which living was denied thee; and either lay it at Sherburne (and if the land continue) or in Exeter-Church, by my father and mother. I can say no more, time and death call me away.

The everlasting God, powerful, infinite, and omnipotent

God, that almighty God, who is goodness it self, the true life and true light keep thee and thine. Have mercy on me, and teach me to forgive my persecutors and false accusers, and send us to meet in his glorious kingdom.

My dear wife farewell. Bless my poor boy. Pray for me, and let my good God hold you both in his arms. Written with the dying hand of sometimes thy husband, but now alas overthrown.

Yours that was, but now not my own.

WR

Alan Turing to Norman Routledge, February 1952

A heartbreaking letter from the time when homosexuality was illegal in the UK. Alan Turing was the computer scientist, mathematician and cryptographer who had played a crucial role in breaking the Nazi Enigma code during the war at Bletchley Park and in developing the Turing test to measure artificial intelligence.

In 1952, Turing was living in Manchester, where he began a relationship with a young man, Arnold Murray. When Murray was burgled, Turing inadvertently revealed his homosexuality during the police investigation, resulting in prosecution for both men for 'gross indecency' under the Criminal Law Amendment Act 1885 then used to prosecute homosexuals. Turing pleaded guilty, facing no time in prison provided he underwent a hormonal treatment similar to chemical castration that helped destroy him. This letter to his friend, the mathematician Norman Routledge, indicates the level of anxiety and misery that he is suffering. He committed suicide by biting into a cyanide-poisoned apple on 8 June 1954.

Homosexuality was decriminalized in 1967 but it was only in 2017 that the 'Turing law' formally pardoned Turing and other homosexuals persecuted under the old laws.

My dear Norman,

I've now got myself into the kind of trouble that I have always considered to be quite a possibility for me, though I have usually rated it at about 10:1 against. I shall shortly be pleading guilty to a charge of sexual offences with a young man. The story of how it all came to be found out is a long and fascinating one, which I shall have to make into a short story one day, but haven't the time to tell you now. No doubt I shall emerge from it all a different man, but quite who I've not found out.

Glad you enjoyed broadcast. Jefferson certainly was rather disappointing though. I'm afraid that the following syllogism may be used by some in the future.

Turing believes machines think
Turing lies with men
Therefore machines do not think

   Yours in distress, Alan

Che Guevara to Fidel Castro, 1 April 1965

The two heroes of the Cuban Revolution. Guevara was a handsome Argentine doctor who, after a motorcycle trip throughout Latin America, joined up with Fidel and Raul Castro, to lead the Cuban Revolution. In the battle to overthrow dictator Fulgencio Batista, Guevara served as a commander of reckless courage and outstanding organisational skills alongside the Castro brothers. They took the capital in 1959. In power, Che oversaw the firing squads that killed 'war criminals', trained the army, and ran the agricultural economy, dominated by sugarcane, as well as steering Cuba into an alliance with the Communist Soviet Union.

Guevara was instrumental in inviting the Soviets to place missiles on the island directed at America, which demanded their removal.

Faced with nuclear war with America in the Missile Crisis, the Soviets withdrew them. Guevara and Castro had been willing to risk nuclear apocalypse. Disillusioned with the Soviet betrayal and perhaps with Castro's dominance, Che seeks new adventure, new revolutions to serve and writes this letter of goodbye.

Guevara then vanishes – first to fight in Congo and then, leaving a letter to his children – 'grow up as good revolutionaries' – to Bolivia. There, aged thirty-nine, he was captured and summarily executed by a CIA-advised rightist militia.

Fidel:

At this moment I remember many things: when I met you in Maria Antonia's house, when you proposed I come along, all the tensions involved in the preparations. One day they came by and asked who should be notified in case of death, and the real possibility of it struck us all. Later we knew it was true, that in a revolution one wins or dies (if it is a real one). Many comrades fell along the way to victory.

Today everything has a less dramatic tone, because we are more mature, but the event repeats itself. I feel that I have fulfilled the part of my duty that tied me to the Cuban revolution in its territory, and I say farewell to you, to the comrades, to your people, who now are mine.

I formally resign my positions in the leadership of the party, my post as minister, my rank of commander, and my Cuban citizenship. Nothing legal binds me to Cuba. The only ties are of another nature – those that cannot be broken as can appointments to posts.

Reviewing my past life, I believe I have worked with sufficient integrity and dedication to consolidate the revolutionary triumph. My only serious failing was not having had more confidence in you from the first moments in the Sierra Maestra, and not having understood quickly enough your qualities as a leader and a revolutionary.

I have lived magnificent days, and at your side I felt the pride of belonging to our people in the brilliant yet sad days of the Caribbean [Cuban Missile] crisis. Seldom has a statesman been more brilliant as you were in those days. I am also proud of having followed you without hesitation, of having identified with your way of thinking and of seeing and appraising dangers and principles.

Other nations of the world summon my modest efforts of assistance. I can do that which is denied you due to your responsibility as the head of Cuba, and the time has come for us to part.

You should know that I do so with a mixture of joy and sorrow. I leave here the purest of my hopes as a builder and the dearest of those I hold dear. And I leave a people who received me as a son. That wounds a part of my spirit. I carry to new battlefronts the faith that you taught me, the revolutionary spirit of my people, the feeling of fulfilling the most sacred of duties: to fight against imperialism wherever it may be. This is a source of strength, and more than heals the deepest of wounds.

I state once more that I free Cuba from all responsibility, except that which stems from its example. If my final hour finds me under other skies, my last thought will be of this people and especially of you. I am grateful for your teaching and your example, to which I shall try to be faithful up to the final consequences of my acts . . .

I am not sorry that I leave nothing material to my wife and children; I am happy it is that way. I ask nothing for them, as the state will provide them with enough to live on and receive an education.

I would have many things to say to you and to our people, but I feel they are unnecessary. Words cannot express what I would like them to, and there is no point in scribbling pages.

Robert Ross to More Adey, 14 December 1900

By the time Oscar Wilde was released from hard prison labour for ho-mosexuality, his career was destroyed and his health wrecked. Travelling on the continent at the turn of the nineteenth century, he was working on his poem *The Ballad of Reading Gaol* – 'Yet each man kills the thing he loves' – about the hanging of a murderer. He also handed Robbie Ross, his executor, *De Profundis*, a public letter of reproach addressed to his lover and nemesis, Lord Alfred 'Bosie' Douglas. After a short reunion with Bosie, Wilde returned to Paris, living at the dire Hôtel d'Alsace in Saint-Germain – 'My wallpaper and I are fighting a duel to the death,' he remarked. 'One of us has got to go.' Here his suppurating ear, which had troubled him for a while, became fatal meningitis.

Robbie Ross had always been his most devoted friend: when Wilde came out of jail, Ross alone in a sullen crowd had taken off his hat: 'Men have gone to heaven for smaller things than that,' Wilde wrote in *De Profundis*. Now Ross and another loyal friend, Reggie Turner, are present at this, Wilde's last scene.

During my absence Reggie went every day to see Oscar, and wrote me short bulletins. Oscar went out several times with him driving, and seemed much better. I had decided that when I had moved my mother to Menton on the following Friday, I would go to Paris, but on the Wednesday evening, at five-thirty, I got a telegram from Reggie saying 'Almost hopeless'. I just caught the express and arrived in Paris at 10.20 in the morning.

Dr Tucker informed me that Oscar could not live for more than two days. His appearance was very painful. He was trying to speak. He was conscious that people were in the room, and raised his hand when I asked him whether he understood. I then went in search of a priest, and after great difficulty found father Cuthbert Dunn, of the Passionists, who came with me at once and administered Baptism and

Extreme Unction – Oscar could not take the Eucharist.
You know I have always promised to bring a priest and I
feel rather guilty that I had so often dissuaded him from
becoming a Catholic, but you know my reasons for doing
so . . . Reggie and I slept at the hotel that night in a room
upstairs. We were called twice by the nurse, who thought
Oscar was actually dying. At about 5.30 in the morning a
complete change came over him, the lines of the face altered,
and I believe what is called the death rattle began, but I
had never heard anything like it before; it sounded like the
horrible turning of a crank, and it never ceased until the end.
Foam and blood came from his mouth, and had to be wiped
away by someone standing by him all the time. At 12 o'clock
I went out to get some food, Reggie mounting guard. He
went out at 12.30. From 1 o'clock we did not leave the room;
the painful noise from the throat became louder and louder.
Reggie and myself destroyed letters to keep ourselves from
breaking down. The nurse was out, and the proprietor of
the hotel had come to take her place; at 1.45 the time of his
breathing altered. I went to the bedside and held his hand,
his pulse began to flutter. He heaved a deep sigh, the only
natural one I had heard since I arrived, the limbs seemed
to stretch involuntarily, the breathing became fainter; he
passed away at 10 minutes to 2 p.m. exactly.

After washing and winding the body, and removing the
appalling debris which has to be burnt, Reggie and myself
and the proprietor started for the Mairie to make the official
declarations.

I'm glad to say dear Oscar looked calm and dignified,
just as he did when he came out of prison. Around his neck
was the blessed rosary which you gave me, and on the
breast, a Franciscan medal given me by one of the nuns. An
unsuccessful photograph of Oscar was taken by Maurice
Gilbert at my request but the flashlight did not work properly.

I can scarcely speak in moderation of the magnanimity, humanity and charity of Dupoirier, the proprietor of the Hôtel d'Alsace. Just before I left Paris Oscar told me he owed him over 190 Pounds. From the day Oscar was laid up he never said anything about it. He was present at Oscar's operation, and attended to him personally every morning, paying for luxuries and necessities ordered by the doctor out of his own pocket.

Reggie Turner had the worst time of all in many ways – he experienced all the horrible uncertainty and the appalling responsibility of which he did not know the extent. It will always be a source of satisfaction to those who were very fond of Oscar, that he had someone like Reggie near him during his last days while he was articulate and sensible of kindness and attention.

Lucrezia Borgia to Leo X, 22 June 1519

A letter from a woman dying of childbirth to her priest. Its writer was born Lucrezia Borgia, daughter of the degenerate Pope Alexander VI (born Rodrigo Borgia) and sister of the merciless Cesare. Elected Pope in 1492, Rodrigo immediately began to enjoy the riches and pleasures of the papacy and to promote his family's prosperity with more shame-lessness and bloodletting than was customary. His eldest son was murdered – most likely by his second son Cesare, who soon became a duke, killing any and all opponents.

Their sister Lucrezia was beautiful, but regarded by many as a she-devil, tainted by the family's crimes. Her husbands and lovers were variously strangled, poisoned or found floating in the Tiber; and she was said to have had a child by either her father or her brother, who then forced her to marry the future Duke of Este.

When father and brother died, Lucrezia was finally freed of her poisonous family and lived on as duchess d'Este for fifteen respectable years. Now, at thirty-nine, she gives birth to a daughter but realises that a post-natal infection has doomed her. She dies two days after writing this to the pope.

Most Holy Father and Honoured Master

With all respect, I kiss your Holiness's feet and commend myself in all humility to your holy mercy. Having suffered for more than two months, early on the morning of the 14th of the present, as it pleased God, I gave birth to a daughter, and hoped then to find relief from my sufferings, but I did not, and shall be compelled to pay my debt to nature. So great is the favour which our merciful Creator has shown me, that I approach the end of life with pleasure, knowing that, in a few hours, after receiving for the last time all the holy sacraments of the Church, I shall be released. Having arrived at this moment, I desire as a Christian, although I am a sinner, to ask your Holiness, in your mercy, to give me all possible spiritual consolation and your Holiness's blessing for my soul. Therefore I offer myself to you in all humility and commend my husband and my children, all of whom are your servants, to your Holiness's mercy.

Your Holiness's humble servant,
Lucrezia d'Este

Hadrian to Antoninus Pius – and his soul, 10 July AD 138

No farewell letter from a dying man to his friends could be more elegant than this one. When he writes this elegy for the departure of his soul, Hadrian is dying at his villa at Baiae.

One of the most gifted men to become emperor of Rome, he was a writer, poet, architect and a restless traveller – in fact, the most travelled of all Roman princeps. He helped design exquisite architecture such as his villa, as well as the Pantheon and his own mausoleum in Rome, the Castel Sant'Angelo. He was married, but his great love was his male lover Antinous; when he died young, Hadrian had him deified. But he was also a ruthless ruler, executing senators and relatives suspected of treason or driving them to suicide, while his suppression of the Jewish revolt of Simon Bar Kokhba was savage.

Now dying, he writes to his chosen successor and adopted son Antoninus Pius: 'Emperor Caesar Hadrian Augustus to Antoninus, greeting. Above all I want you to know that I am being released from my life neither before my time or unreasonably or piteously nor unexpectedly nor with faculties impaired even though I shall almost seem to do injury to you who are by my side . . . my father fell ill at the age of forty so I have lived twice again as long as him and reached the same age as my mother . . .' And he most probably includes in the letter this whimsical goodbye to his own soul, one of the best salutations to death ever written:

ANIMULA, VAGULA, BLANDULA,
HOSPES COMESQUE CORPORIS,
QUAE NUNC ABIBIS IN LOCA
PALLIDULA, RIGIDA, NUDULA,
NEC, UT SOLES, DABIS IOCOS

Little soul, little wanderer, little charmer,
body's guest and companion,
to what places will you set out for now?
To darkling, cold and gloomy ones –
and you won't make your usual jokes.

Acknowledgements

I want to thank my colleagues and friends who have helped with brilliant ideas for this book: Tom Holland, Andrew Roberts, Jonathan Foreman, Kate Jarvis, Dr Lorenza Smith, F. M. Eloischari and my very well-read mother, April Sebag-Montefiore. Special thanks to Jan Christian Mollestad for telling me the real story of Leonard Cohen's letter to Marianne and allowing me to quote his words. Thank you to my publishers David Shelley and Holly Harley and to my agents Georgina Capel, Rachel Conway, Irene Baldoni and my movie and TV agent Simon Shaps. Special thanks to my daughter Lily for helping me choose the letters on an exciting voyage through my library. Thanks to Alex Larman for additional research. And as always thanks to my darling wife Santa, my daughter Lily and my son Sasha.

Copyright Acknowledgements

The author and publishers gratefully acknowledge permission to reprint copyright material in this collection as follows. Every effort has been made to trace copyright holders and to obtain their permission for the use of copyright material. The publisher apologises for any errors or omissions in the below list and would be grateful if notified of any corrections that should be incorporated in future reprints or editions of this book.

p.4 Frida Kahlo to Diego Rivera, undated: *The Diary of Frida Kahlo: An Intimate Self-Portrait*, Frida Kahlo, edited by Phyllis Freeman. © Banco de Mexico Diego Rivera Frida Kahlo Museums Trust, Mexico, D.F./DACS 2018; p.6 Thomas Jefferson to Maria Cosway, 12 October 1786: Founders Online, National Archives, last modified June 13, 2018 http://founders.archives.gov/documents/Jefferson/01-10-02-0309; p.10 Catherine the Great to Prince Potemkin, c.19 March 1774: *Great Catherine*, Carolly Erickson, Simon & Schuster, 1994; p.12 James I to the Duke of Buckingham, 17 May 1620: *Letters of King James*, VI & I, ed. G. P. V. Akrigg, University of California Press, 1984; p.13 Vita Sackville-West to Virginia Woolf, 21 January 1926: Excerpts from *The Letters of Virginia Woolf*, Volume 3, edited by Nigel Nicolson and assistant editor. Published by Chatto & Windus. © 1977 Joanne Trautmann © by Quentin Bell and Angelica Garnett, 1977, 1978, 1978, 1980. Reproduced with permission from The Random House Group Ltd; p.15 Between Suleiman the Magnificent and Hurrem Sultan, c. 1530s: *The Imperial Harem: Women and Sovereignty in the Ottoman Empire*, Leslie Peirce, Oxford University Press, 1991, p.64; p.19 Anaïs Nin to Henry Miller, c.August 1932:

Tse-tung Thought, a Red Guard Publication. Transcription by the Maoist Documentation Project; p.113 Josip Broz Tito to Stalin, 1948: *Stalin: A Biography*, Robert Service, Macmillan, 2004, p.592. Reproduced with permission from Macmillan; p.117 Theobald von Bethman-Hollwegg to Leopold Berchtold, 6 July 1914: *The 'Blank Check'*, World War Document Archive. http://www.gwpda.org/1914/blankche.html GWDPA.orgH; p.119 Harry Truman to Irv Kupcinet, 5 August 1963: Truman Papers, Post-Presidential File. Chicago Sun-Times. Harry S. Truman Library; p.133 Captain A.D. Chater to his mother, Christmas 1914: The Family of Captain A. D. Chater; p.153 Georg von Hülsen to Emil von Görtz, 1892: *The Kaiser and his Court*, John C. G. Röhl. Cambridge University Press, 2008, p.16. Translated from Eulenbergs Korrespondenz, II, p.953. Reproduced with permission from Cambridge University Press; p.154 Marquis de Sade 'to the stupid villains who torment me', 1783: *Selected Letters of Marquis de Sade*, edited by Margaret Crosland, Peter Owen, 1965. Reproduced with permission from Peter Owen Publishers UK; p.156 Between Alexandra and Nicholas II, 14 December 1916: *The Romanovs: 1613-1918*, Simon Sebag Montefiore, Weidenfeld & Nicolson, 2016; p.163 Maria Theresa to Marie Antoinette, 30 July 1775: *Secrets of Marie-Antionette: A Collection of Letters*, edited by Oliver Bernier, Fromm, 1986, p.172. Reproduced with permission from Olivier Bernier; p.164 Mahatma Gandhi to Hitler, 24 December 1940: *Letter to Adolf Hitler*, As at Wardha, December 24, 1940; p.167 Abraham Lincoln to Ulysses S. Grant, 13 July 1863: *Collected Works of Abraham Lincoln*, edited by Roy P. Basler et al., Abraham Lincoln Association, 1953; p.169 Jacqueline Kennedy to Nikita Khrushchev, 1 December 1963: *The Death of a President*, November 20-November 25, 1963 William Manchester, 1963, pp. 653-654. John F Kennedy Presidential Library; p.172 Émile Zola to Félix Faure, 13 January 1898: *L'Aurore*, Jan. 13, 1898, translated by Chameleon Translations. p.183 Emmeline Pankhurst to the Women's Social and Political Union, 10 January 1913: National Archives;

p.185 Rosa Parks to Jessica Mitford, 26 February 1956: Rosa Parks Papers: General Correspondence, 2006; Alphabetical file; Mitford, *Jessica "Decca" Treuhaft, letter from Parks, 1956* Rosa Parks™ Used with permission from The Rosa and Raymond Parks Institute for Self-Development. All rights reserved; p.186 Nelson Mandela to Winnie Mandela, 2 April 1969: *The Prison Letters of Nelson Mandela*, Liveright Publishing Corp., 2018, in cooperation with the Estate of Nelson Mandela and the Nelson Mandela Foundation in South Africa. Reproduced with permission from The Estate of Nelson Mandela; p.189 Abram Hannibal to Peter the Great, 5 March 1722: *Hannibal: The Moor of Petersburg*, Hugh Barnes, Profile Books, 2006. Courtesy of Profile Books; p.190 Between Simón Bolívar, Manuela Sáenz and James Thorne, 3 July 1822: *Bolivar: The Epic Life of the Man Who Liberated South America*, Marie Arana, Weidenfeld & Nicolson, 2014; p.203 Babur to his son Humayun, 11 January 1529: *An Unpublished Testament of Babur*, N. C. Mehta, The Twentieth Century, 1936, p.340; p.210 Alexander Pushkin to Jacob von Heeckeren, 25 January 1837: *Pushkin*, Ernest J. Simmons, Cambridge, Mass.: Harvard University Press, Copyright © 1937 by the President and Fellows of Harvard College; p.215 Stalin to Valery Mezhlauk, April 1930: *Stalin: The Court of the Red Tsar*, Simon Sebag Montefiore, Weidenfeld & Nicolson 2010; p.216 Churchill to Roosevelt, 20 May 1940: Reproduced with permission of Curtis Brown Group Ltd on behalf of The Estate of Sir Winston S. Churchill. © The Estate of Winston S. Churchill; p.217 Between Richard I and Saladin, October–November 1191: *Saladin and the Fall of the Kingdom of Jerusalem*, Stanley Lane-Poole, Greenhill Books, 2002. Reproduced with permission; p.221 Niccolò Machiavelli to Francesco Vettori, 3 August 1514: Reprinted from *Machiavelli and His Friend*, edited and translated by James Atkinson & David Sices, with permission from Northern Illinois University Press. Copyright © 2004; p.225 Donald J. Trump to Kim Jong Un, 24 May 2018: *Letter to Chairman Kim Jong U'*, The White House

Statements & Releases, Foreign Policy. Issued on: May 24, 2018 https://www.whitehouse.gov/briefings-statements/letter-chairman-kim-jong-un/; p.232 Simon Bar Kokhba to Yeshua, c.AD 135: *Bar Kockba Letter*, translated by Dr William Bean; p.217 Ammurapi to the king of Alashiya, c.1190 BC: *A New evidence on the last days of Ugarit*, Astour, M. C., Archaeological Institute of America, 1965, p255. Reproduced with permission from the Archaeological Institute of America; p.235 Bolívar to Juan José Flores, 9 November 1830: *Bolivar*, Marie Arana, Weidenfeld & Nicolson, 2014; p.239 Leonard Cohen to Marianne Ihlen, July 2016: Reproduced with permission from the Estate of Leonard Cohen; p.240 'Henriette' to Giacomo Casanova, autumn 1749: *The Memoirs of Jacques Casanova de Seingalt,* Volume. 2 "To Paris and Prison", Giacomo Casanova, Start Publishing LLC, 2013; p.241 Churchill to his wife Clementine, 1915: Reproduced with permission of Curtis Brown Group Ltd on behalf of The Estate of Sir Winston S. Churchill © The Estate of Winston S. Churchill; p.247 Franz Kafka to Max Brod, June 1924: *The Trial*, Franz Kafka, translated by Willa and Edwin Muir, Secker, © 1986). All Kafka Material is copyrighted by Schocken Books Inc, New York. Translation and Notes © Schocken Books Inc. 1958, 1977 Reproduced with permission from The Random House Group Ltd.; p.251 Alan Turing to Norman Routledge, February 1952: Unpublished writings of A. M. Turing © copyright The Provost and Scholars of King's College Cambridge 2018. Reproduced with permission; p.252 Che Guevara to Fidel Castro, 1 April 1965: *The Bolivian Diary of Ernesto Che Guevara*, Ernesto Che Guevara, translated by Michael J. Taber, Pathfinder, 1994, p.81. El Diario del Che en Bolivia copyright (c) 1987, 1988 by Editoria Politica. Copyright © 1994 by Pathfinder Press. Reprinted by permission; p.258 Hadrian to Antoninus Pius – and to his soul, 10 July AD 138: *Hadrian: The Restless Emperor*, Anthony Richard Birley, Psychology Press, 1997, p. 301. Copyright © 1997 Psychology Press. Reproduced with permission from Taylor & Francis Group.